NOT ONLY IN ISOLATION

My First 20 years 1928-1948

Molly Van Cleemput née Britten

authorHOUSE®

AuthorHouse™ UK Ltd.
500 Avebury Boulevard
Central Milton Keynes, MK9 2BE
www.authorhouse.co.uk
Phone: 08001974150

First published by AuthorHouse   9/9/2010

ISBN: 978-1-4520-5432-2 (sc)

This book is printed on acid-free paper.

Dedication

To my husband Marcel for the help he has given me since this book was just an idea.

Also to my daughters Patrice and Ginette for their continued interest and unfailing encouragement.

To my Grand daughters Karen and laura for their great interest.

Prologue

My life started in Northampton on the 15th of March 1928 – the same year talking pictures were introduced but I deny any connection! I was born at Colwyn Road Nursing Home and was in fact, the last baby to be born there. Most of the nurses were Irish and as I was born so near to St Patrick's Day they pleaded with Mum to call me Patricia. She agreed but as my many great aunts shortened it to Patty or Patsy she promptly started to call me Molly. My father often called me Molly-Polly or Mollypop.

My father was William James Britten, my mother Nora Britten (nee Ives) and I was their second child, their first was my big brother Geoffrey James, born November 14th 1923 and their youngest, my baby brother, Brian William, born February 10th 1936.

As a baby in family group with my brother Geoff behind me

My parents, Nora & Bill

We lived at 43 Lincoln Road, in St James, which was a three bedroomed, terraced house with a long garden, or so it seemed to me, which backed on to similar long gardens in Spencer Street. Beyond that, to the side, we had a view over the Six Fields. There was no bathroom in the house so baths were taken in a tin bath in the kitchen in warm weather and in front of a fire in the living room when it was cold. The toilet was outside which made for very quick visits in cold weather. No modern toilet paper, just squares of newspaper hung up with string.

We had a front room that was only used on special occasions; in fact I felt I was trespassing when I dared to creep in. The other room was much more homely with comfortable easy chairs as well as the dining table and chairs. There was also a piano which, as both my parents played, was well used.

Chapter One

Early Years

I have been told by my parents that my life was uneventful until I was about 18 months old when I contracted meningitis. The tale goes that alarm bells didn't ring until Mum found my back was as "stiff as a board" and then a doctor was sent for in a hurry. He promptly got me to the hospital and all sorts of things were done to me which, thankfully, I don't remember. Mum says that my screams were heard echoing through the corridors and they were told I probably wouldn't live. I did though, against all odds, and had no nasty after effects. She also told me that up to that illness I had lovely dark curly hair which the meningitis caused to fall out. Alas it grew back fair, fine and straight which was really a pity as I would have much preferred the dark hair to go with my blue eyes. Still, it was a small price to pay to continue living!

Another tale told to me of my childhood was the time I developed a whitlow on my finger. My mother was treating it and, after applying numerous bread poultices, had got it to the point of needing to be lanced when in came my Nan Britten who told Mum that she knew a way to save the doctor's fee. Trustingly she surrendered me to her care when to her horror Nan told me to put my finger on the floor and then trod hard on it. Again I am thankful I don't remember it.

My first real memories, though a bit disjointed, started at about three years old and consisted mainly of dancing classes. I was taken to Grace Wooton's Dancing School, which at that time was held at a big house in St. James Main Road, only a few minutes away from home. Even at that tender age I was fitted with block ballet shoes and taught to dance on pointes - cotton wool was stuffed into the toes to stop it being too painful. The first part of each lesson was to go on pointe all round the studio and the applause from the attendant mothers' was great if the exercise was accomplished without a stop. That studio circuit seemed endless at first but pretty soon it became second nature to go up on my toes, in fact, much to my mother's annoyance, I used to do it in my smart patent leather ankle strap shoes, in the street or any other place if the fancy took me. I remember a few smacks for scuffing the toes of my best shoes. Another torture devised by Miss Wootton was the 'splits'. We had to go down as far as we could and then she would go round the class and push hard on the shoulders until she couldn't see any space between body and floor. I wince even now when I think of it! It didn't stop with that though as once down in the splits all sorts of other contortions followed. Yet another regular exercise was to get down on our tummies and arch our backs in order to touch the back of our heads with our feet. Needless to say, we were 'helped' with that too!

Little ballerina aged 3

Strangely enough I quite enjoyed the lessons except for one that sticks in my memory. We were learning a dance for a show which required the baby class to be toy soldiers and at one point we were wounded and had to do a stiff leg walk. Again the studio circuit came into play and we had to practice this walk round the room until we got it right and in time to the music. For some reason I suddenly got stage fright and refused to do it. I took to my mother's lap and tried to stay there but eventually I was persuaded to give it a go and once I got going I was able to do it without a hitch - relief all round! That was my only attack of stage fright and later I was in shows at the New Theatre with no problems.

One dance I can remember very well was as a butterfly. I loved the costume - the wings especially. My granddad, Papa painted the design in gold on the gauze and I was really happy with it. The dance started with four groups of four of us sleeping with wings folded over heads and one by one the groups stirred, woke up and began to dance. I was a bit afraid I would miss my cue and peeped over one wing to make sure I didn't. That must have been an "Ah" factor!

Mum at the back, Nan Ives, Uncle George and Papa

Another favourite costume was the Pierrot which was chequered in brown and orange with stiff ruffs round the neck, ankles and wrists. A little skull cap with bobbles at the front completed the outfit. The dance was quite energetic and required lots of splits etc. A studio photo taken proves that I had learnt to get right down.

Little Pierrot

I can remember very well having that photo taken in Jeromes studio in the Drapery. It was a cold day and I wasn't very happy to have to strip off my warm clothes and dress first in my tutu and then in the Pierrot costume, both quite flimsy.

Yet another costume was used in a scene for Wash Day Blues.

Washday Blues , I'm at the first right

I have a small photograph of me, taken at Auto Portraits and I was dressed in a fur looking coat and woolly leggings. I was probably about three years of age and I don't really remember the session but I don't look very happy about it. The photo size is like today's passport photos you can take yourself, in a booth.

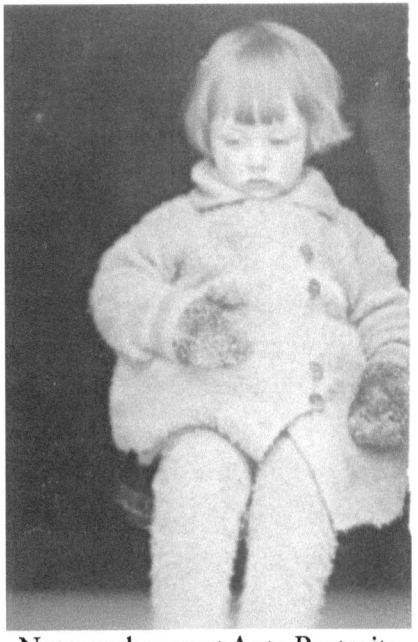

Not very happy at Auto Portraits

I can recall one other item of clothing from about that time. It was a pair of brown leather gaiters which covered my legs from the foot to just over the knee. They went over the shoes and were held in place by a piece of elastic under the instep. They were fastened all the way by small round buttons and I believe my mother used a button hook to do them up.

My mother was very keen for me to learn to read and from an early age she bought me a weekly comic called "Chicks Own". She used to read it to me at first but at the same time encouraged me to spell out words for myself. That particular comic, as I remember, was geared to teaching children to read, as all the longer words were hyphenated into syllables. For example chicken would be printed as chick-en, puppy would become pup-py and so on thus making it easier. The stories were mostly as captions under pictures and I always looked forward to the day that comic came out so that I could follow the adventures of the little animals. I always got an Annual in my Christmas stocking, actually a pillowcase!, and of course The Chicks Own Annual was a must and by the time I graduated to Tiger Tim comics I could cope with most of the reading myself, this gave me a good start when I went to school.

My mother was great on helping my schooling as she also used to buy me copy writing books. These had first words, and further on in the book sentences printed and spaces under them so that they could be faithfully copied. There were grid lines to show how high each letter, and parts of the letter should be and of course, this type of work also taught spelling quite painlessly. I spent many happy hours working on these books and reading my comics and annuals but although I developed a great love of reading, shared by all the family, my hand writing never amounted to much. It was fine whilst I was at the printing stage but later on, even with the aid of the more advanced books, my "joined-up" writing left a lot to be desired. It was even more ruined at the Northampton School for Girls when we were made to abandon any 'style' we had, to conform to the school idea of good handwriting i.e. no loops on letters.

I don't really remember being with my older brother Geoff much at this early age. He was almost 4 years older than me and was sent to a nursery school in Bowden Road, always called the Tin School, before starting at Spencer Infants where I was to follow in his footsteps when I was 4½ years old. I was really looking forward to starting school and remember my first day there. Mum took me and we went through the covered lobby to see the classrooms situated all round a quadrangle, sheltered by a covered veranda. I thought it was all very pretty and wasn't at all bothered at being left there. We, the new children, were met by the head mistress, Miss Buswell, and shown where to hang our coats in the cloakroom. Then we were taken to our first classroom and introduced to our teacher, Miss Smith, a plumpish, kindly lady who soon settled us in. At the mid-morning break we had a small bottle of milk to drink. They were stubby little bottles that had a cardboard top set into the neck. We had to push at a perforated hole to open it for the straw and, as you might imagine, quite often, could be pushed in too quickly to control, resulting in a jet of milk shooting out and going down the front of your clothes. It was very funny to see it happen to one of the others but not quite so funny to have it happen to yourself. Milk can make clothes a bit stiff and, on a hot day, not very sweet smelling by the end of the school day! Once we had drunk our milk we were sent into the playground at the back of the school - it seemed enormous but I soon enjoyed getting to know new friends and we had some good times there. The toilet block was in the playground, one part for boys and the other for girls. We were expected to 'go' during the play time so there was usually quite a queue and as the door to each cubicle had no latch, each of us took it in turn to guard the door. One or two girls guarded the main entrance to the girls' block as, quite often, the boys would try to peek in!

We had games lessons in the playground too as well as 'drill' which involved a lot of marching and usually included an exercise where we started marching and had to keep an eye on an appointed leader who made the change to running, skipping or hopping. It caused a bit of a pile-up if someone failed to notice the change. As for the other lessons, I can remember that we first started our writing lessons on slates using chalk and when judged to be proficient enough we graduated to pencils and exercise books. Mum had done such good ground work with me that I was soon promoted. We had arithmetic (sums) lessons and were taught our multiplication tables parrot fashion. For reading we had simple picture books to start with and learned the words printed underneath. Sometimes we read in unison but from time to time we had to go to the teacher and read to her on our own. From doing this she moved each child on to the next book according to ability. We had regular spelling tests, the teacher reading out the words which we then had to write in our books. If we got any wrong we had to copy out the correct spelling 5 or 10 times, according to how many times the word had been mis-spelt in previous tests. The best bit of the day, in the first class only, was the last part when we had to put away our books and settle down to listen to the teacher reading a story - I loved that. All in all I was very happy at Spencer Infants and I can't remember any difficulties with the work, even arithmetic although, unfortunately, in my later school years, maths was to become quite a struggle for me. Perhaps my first teachers were better at their job - who knows! The other teachers I remember were Miss Linnell, a severe looking lady with spectacles, who took the second from top class, and Miss Agutter, who took the top class. She was much loved and as well as teaching my two brothers and myself, she later moved to St. James Infant school and there taught both my daughters.

We never saw much of Miss Buswell, I think she only emerged from her office for school assemblies and to take classes in another teacher's absence.

The only very slight cloud on my horizon was the often repeated question 'Are you going to be as clever as your brother?' I got very good with the angelic smile and the answer 'I'll try.' I did try, very hard, but never did get any where near as clever as him.

One truly awful thing happened when I was in Miss Agutter's class. Each school day ended with class prayers and during the last part of the last lesson I felt I really had to go to the toilet but when I raised my hand and asked to go I was told to wait until the end of prayers. Alas I had left it too long and as we leaned forward to pray a puddle started to form on my seat! I was absolutely mortified and ran from the class room as soon as I could. Nobody, teacher or child ever mentioned it, but I never forgot the shame of 'wetting my knickers'.

The school day was from 9am to 12pm and then home for lunch, going back for the afternoon session from 2pm to 4pm. There was always a hot meal ready at lunchtime and after walking about half a mile home I was ready for it. Mum took and fetched me for a few days but after that I went in the care of the 'big girls' of Lincoln Road and when I got just a little bit older I was allowed to make the journey on my own. Life was a lot safer for children then although I still had to negotiate my way across St James Main Road, Harlestone Road and Spencer Bridge Road. I was taught the safer crossing points and it was stressed that I should only use them and no other, but if I felt unsure I could ask an adult (a lady) to see me across. There were no 'pelican' crossings or 'lollipop' persons then, even their forerunners the Belisha Beacons were yet to arrive. It was a case of seeing a space in the traffic and running across.

There was only one other warning that I remember getting, apart from the continual one of behaving and doing as I was told, this was when Mum got very serious and told me that if a man on a bicycle ever offered to give me a ride home, I was to say firmly, no thank you, and on no account accept. She never told me why, even though I asked, and I thought to myself that if he ever did, I would go with him. I figured that I could easily jump off the crossbar when I got near to home and it would save a long walk. Just as well I never met him!

Most of the children I knew went to Sunday School every Sunday afternoon and, as both my parents were 'Chapel', I was duly enrolled at Doddridge Chapel in St James Main Road, at an early age. It was a lovely school and I thoroughly enjoyed it all. We started off altogether with hymns and prayers and then went off to our various age related groups to listen to Bible stories, finishing again altogether with closing prayers and hymns. One of my presents in the past had been a small illustrated Bible and I was convinced that the coloured pictures in it were photographs so when a Sunday School teacher was describing Jesus to us and said that people believed he had a beard, I quickly assured her that he really did - I had his picture in my Bible!

We had a summer Sunday School outing each year and I suppose that other schools joined us for the event as a great number of children met up at Castle Station on the great day. We piled on the train and I thought we had gone miles but many years later I realised that we had, in fact, gone on a very slow train for the few miles to Blisworth. Once there, we were taken to a nearby field where we played organised games and finally sat down to a picnic tea. We were all very tired and happy when we got on the train to go home to our parents. I don't know if we went to Blisworth every year, I suspect we did, as that is the only venue that sticks in my mind.

An off-shoot to Sunday School was a Monday evening meeting, held in the Chapel, of the Band Of Hope, a Temperance Society. This was great fun and most of the children in our streets went. We were first of all given a lecture on the evils of drink and shown posters to illustrate the point. One I particularly remember, held up by the usual enthusiastic speaker, was a copy of a poster on all the bill boards at the time, showing a glass of beer with the caption underneath "Beer is Best". He told us that the caption was only part of the message and then unrolled the last bit of his poster so that it read

Beer is Best
LEFT ALONE!

It made a huge impression on me and every time we passed the advert on the hoardings, I used to quote the full message. I finally exhausted my parents' patience and was told they never wanted to hear it again!

After the lectures we were treated to a concert of local talent which usually amused us. One memorable evening one of the acts was dances performed by Grace Wootton, my ex-dancing teacher, and during one of the more energetic dances her skirt flew up and revealed she had forgotten to put on anything underneath. You can imagine the roar that went up but, to her credit, even though you could tell by her face that she realised what she had done, she finished the dance. I felt so sorry for her but she got a huge round of applause.

Another memory was when, after I'd been in bed for a while, I was wakened by my parents, wrapped up in a blanket and carried across the fields to see a spectacular fire. It was at a big firm, Travis and Arnold, who at that time had large stores of wood, and, as we got nearer, the sky was lit up by the flames and the crackling noise of the wood burning in the warehouses, together with explosions was extremely loud. We had joined a large crowd of people who had come to see the spectacle and all had come via the Six Fields as the roads to the factory would have been blocked by the fire engines. We could see firemen fighting to put out the flames and it was all very dramatic. The flames were reflected in the river that was in front of where we were standing, which made the sight even more amazing. We stood there for hours and even when we left, the fire was still burning.

I wasn't very old then but I have never seen such a fire since.

Whilst living at Lincoln Road, music seemed to play a large part in our life. Mum was always singing or humming about the house as she worked and even now I think of her when I hear the song Vijla, from The Merry Widow by Lehar: I think that must have been one of her favourites. Both Mum and Dad belonged to a choir before they married so they knew a lot of songs from musical operas and lots of ballads. They both played the piano and sometimes played duets together. Mum had a lighter touch than Dad who used to love playing rousing marching songs, thumping the left hand and with left foot firmly down on the loud pedal. He played the Anvil Chorus, William Tell overture and the like with great enthusiasm. I think the way he played was called vamping, frowned on by the purists but he could always play a tune by ear and rarely used music sheets

When I was older Mum and Dad thought I should be taught to play the piano and Uncle George, Mum's brother, offered to give me lessons. When, after learning lots of scales and other basics, I was ready to learn to read and play from sheet music. After practising a piece for the whole week I found that, without meaning to, I had memorised it and could play it by heart. Uncle George realised what was happening and was not pleased. He would stop me playing and ask me to point on the music sheet where I had got to. I don't know who was most surprised, him or me, when I pointed to the right spot as on my part it was pure guess work. I wasn't really enjoying the lessons and decided I didn't want to go for any more. I know Mum was disappointed but suspect Uncle George wasn't.

As well as piano music at home we always listened to the Palm Court Orchestra on the wireless, the name 'radio' came much later, as well as theatre organ music by Reginald Dixon, Reginald Fforte and later, Sandy McPherson. There were Variety Programmes that also featured music, both by orchestras or singers like Anne Zeigler and Webster Booth. One of many comediennes was Jeanette de Casalis who always finished her act by acting as a very dithery, harassed Mrs Feather, speaking on the telephone. Elsie and Doris Waters were firm favourites too with their comic sketches as well as Stainless Stephen who would read passages and make funny noises for the different punctuation marks.

I always enjoyed listening to Harry Hemsley with his imaginary family, Johnny, Elsie, Winnie and baby Horace. He told stories with the 'family' joining in but little Horace could only use baby babbling noises and Harry would always ask "What did Horace say Elsie?" Elsie would then translate.

My favourite, as was the favourite of most children, was Children's Hour with Uncle Mac. There was Toy Town with Larry the Lamb and his friends on the farm. A gently educational Romany took us on imaginary walks in the country describing the fruits of the hedgerows and the animals, wild as well as those on the farms. He made everything seem so real and I never tired of listening to him. When the programme was finished at five to 6, Uncle Mac always closed with "Good night children, everywhere".

A programme from Radio Luxemburg was The Ovaltinies with a very catchy signature tune beginning

We are the Ovaltinies

Happy girls and boys

I joined the Ovaltinies club and treasured the badge for many years. It's mildly annoying that this is all I remember of those broadcasts.

Chapter 2

Celebrations

I realise now that Mum and Dad didn't have much money but I can't remember going short of anything. There was always a birthday party for us with plenty of fun and presents. We must have had longer summers in my childhood because, as far as I remember, even though it is said that one only remembers the sunny days of the past, my birthday parties in mid-March, were nearly always held in the garden. We would play 'ring' games such as 'I sent a letter to my love' and 'The farmer wants a wife' - the latter was great fun ending with the enthusiastic patting of the dog that the nurse wanted! We only went indoors for tea which was always a sumptuous spread of sandwiches followed by tinned fruit with cream, jelly and blancmange with custard and, of course, the grand finale of the Birthday cake with the candles. Fizzy drinks of Tizer or Corona washed it all down. It wasn't obligatory to eat all of it but I think we did!

While our tea 'went down' Dad, the proud owner of a cinematograph, would sometimes project a film for us, using a white sheet as a screen. I remember we saw Felix the cat, a favourite of mine, and some Charlie Chaplin films. For no particular reason I always remember one was called

'A Little Piece of Fluff' which took two reels to tell the story. I told everyone that we were going to see 'A little piece of fluff in two parts'!

Another fairly big event was Bonfire Night, celebrated always on the 5th November and not just the nearest weekend as happens now. I suspect Dad got as much pleasure as us from making a huge bonfire and gathering together a good supply of fireworks for the big night. He and Geoff favoured the 'bangers' but Mum and I, and later my baby brother Brian, enjoyed the pretty ones and the sparklers. Probably my earliest memory of Geoff is of him terrorising me with the banging jumping fire crackers. Maybe it was a fluke but one year he actually managed to get one to chase me up the garden path!

Christmas was a lot of fun too. In the build-up to the big day I would be set to making paper chains. These were made from bundles of multi-coloured strips of gummed paper. I had to lick the edges of each piece to make the first ring and then thread each following ring into the previous one to form a long chain. These were draped round the room with some hung from the light shade in the centre of the room to radiate out to the corners. The chains were renewed each year but a box of more elaborate decorations was brought out too. There were of folded paper between pieces of cardboard which opened out into pretty ruffled balls and bells. When our Christmas tree was brought home there were the tree decorations to carefully lift out of their boxes. They were delicate paper thin glass baubles in many different shapes and some had glittering strands of tinsel draped on them. My favourites were shaped as peacocks with their long shiny 'tails' hanging behind them.

The tree decorations also included little coloured candles in tin holders to clip onto the branches. Occasionally they were lit but only for a short time as they were too dangerous to be left. They were very pretty and the smell of the candle wax, together with the smell of the pine tree, created a lovely festive air.

The Christmas celebrations went on for ages because we were part of a large extended family in those days and all our great-aunts living in Northampton had parties. However it is Nan Ives's that is most memorable. The food at her parties was of course more 'grown-up' and the table groaned under its load of tinned lobster and crab, pork pies, ham, tongue, brawn (ugh!), tomatoes, cucumbers, radishes, water cress, celery and other green salads followed by the fruit and cream, a large trifle as well as the jellies and blancmanges and little fancy cakes but the piece de resistance was always the very grand Christmas cake. This was made a month or two before Christmas, later covered with home-made marzipan and about three layers of Royal icing. Each layer was carefully smoothed, and allowed to dry out before applying the next, and lastly the lovely decorative work. Papa always decorated the cakes and I absolutely adored to watch him apply the lattice work and different coloured rosettes etc, using various nozzles on the icing gun and always finishing them off with 'silver' balls. An added attraction was that he always let me eat dollops of icing! In the months previous, when Nan started her cake, I was usually on hand to sample anything going and my reward for 'helping' to clean the fruit was to be allowed to eat a few handfuls, but I especially enjoyed preparing the candied peel. This came from the grocer in blue paper bags, as did all the dried fruit, and, prior to being chopped, the delicious candy had to be prised from the centre of the peel. This too I was allowed to eat and it was so good. It's no wonder that I developed a sweet tooth!

Christmas Day itself started early after weeks of looking forward to what Father Christmas might bring. I was always sent to bed early on Christmas Eve, this being the only night in the year that I went willingly, and so woke very early in the morning, usually before it was light. The first thing was to feel the pillowcase to see if 'He' had been. Of course he had, so the next thing was to try to identify, by feeling, what he had brought. I was forbidden to turn on the light and had to wait, not very patiently, until daylight dawned before investigating properly. The presents weren't gift wrapped so it was just a matter of pulling out the presents one by one. The big ones were at the top and quite often included my favourite sweet shop. This came looking like a big box that opened up to form the inside of a little shop which was stocked with small jars of sweets on a tiny ledge behind the counter together with little dummy bars and boxes of chocolate, also filled with tiny sweets, in the front of them. There was a set of scales to weigh out the goods and little bags to put them in before handing them to the customers. Quite often I was the only one as the family got tired of the game long before I did, but if that was the case I would weigh everything out, put them in the bags and then tip them back into the jars, thus prolonging the play life of the shop. Of course, in the end, everything was shared and eaten. It was a very strict rule of the family that, whoever had sweets, had to offer them round to all present before taking one ourselves. Sometimes a hard rule to keep and it was always a nice surprise when the offer was declined.

Another present was a book which had a stand up cardboard doll set in the cover. This was easily pressed out and there were pages of paper clothes to be cut out ready to be attached to the doll by tabs. This was not only a Christmas present as I sometimes got a book for a birthday or just bought for me as a treat. I remember one doll I had, depicted Shirley Temple and the clothes she wore in her films. There were tabs on each shoulder and at the waist. These were the easiest but the hardest were the hats which had to have a slit cut out the centre and then fixed over the head. If the slit was too big, the hat slipped down round the neck but if it wasn't big enough, the hat got torn and spoilt. It was quite tricky to get it just right but I enjoyed dressing the dolls with the different outfits.

Another often repeated present was a stencil set, consisting of several stencil cut-outs in stiff waxed card, paints with a little sponge for applying them, together with some wax crayons and sheets of paper on which to make the pictures. I spent many happy hours with all of these.

Plasticine gave me a lot of pleasure too. The slim boxes, decorated with pictures of all the exciting models that could be made, were tightly packed with ridged slabs of different coloured plasticine. Sometimes they were covered in the box with a printed sheet of yet more models. I only succeeded in making little people and animals and I tried to use just one colour for each as I hated to mix the different colours.

There were the annuals, mentioned earlier, and other books, some for reading, some for colouring, some for both, and various other stocking fillers but always, right at the bottom and just as enjoyable as the bigger items, I would find a sugar mouse or pig, a tangerine and a bright new shiny penny. The big presents were kept downstairs and there was the delight of a new doll, a dolls pram, a doll's cot and one year, a small cycle, called a fairy cycle. There was only one big present per year and of course it was always just what we wanted. The year I had a fairy cycle I was really thrilled but the snag was that I couldn't ride it. Dad and Geoff tried to teach me by running alongside holding on to the back of the saddle but as soon as they let go I wobbled and almost fell off. In the end I got on the cycle without them, propped myself against a wall and cycled, rubbing along the wall until I eventually steered into the road. I was triumphantly riding my bike but then came another snag, I didn't know how to stop! I steered up onto the pavement and then against a wall. I stopped by rubbing along it, reversing my starting procedure. I collected a few grazes on my arm but it was worth it.

Geoff had some pretty exciting big presents too and I well remember one - a train set that puffed out real steam! This was achieved by using methylated spirits, not something that would be allowed these days. He had a lot of Meccano and made some very intricate models. One I remember, because he let me play with it, was a crane that could hoist up and lower small loads. He had a chest of drawers in his bedroom and one drawer was full of pieces of meccano.

One Christmas Brian's presents included a clockwork tin plate toy car which had headlights powered by a battery. He took it with him to Nan's party and I remember that he had to stand by while Dad, Geoff, Papa and Uncle George 'demonstrated' how well it worked by running it up and down the passage in the dark. It was quite impressive and Brian showed a lot of patience in letting the adults play with it!

When I was eight I began to doubt the existence of Father Christmas and I told my parents that I didn't believe. They said that if that was the case I wouldn't expect any presents in my stocking whereupon I immediately changed my mind.

In the month of May, 1935, the Silver Jubilee of King George and Queen Mary was celebrated. Towns put up decorations and held thanksgiving services.

In Lincoln Road, as in many small streets of Northampton, a big street party was held. With no traffic in our street to disturb the celebrations, a long table laden with party food was set up in the middle of the road. The street was decorated with flags and bunting and we all wore paper hats. The children of Sharman Road must have joined in as I remember there were lots of us sitting down to enjoy the treat. There were sandwiches followed by fruit, jelly, blancmange, custard and cream, all washed down by various soft drinks. Little decorated cakes were there too for those who still had room for them. The mothers had prepared all the food and they, together with the men folk, waited on the children at table.

After the feast we children were each presented with a souvenir mug. The very young ones received a spoon with a coloured metal crown on the handle.

The tables were cleared and we then played lots of games, supervised mainly by the men whilst the ladies dealt with clearing the tables. We played until it was dark and most of us were then taken home and put to bed. It was a truly wonderful day.

The following January in 1936 wasn't such a happy occasion. The adults had been sad faced for a while because it had been announced that "The King's life was drawing to a close" but then one morning it was announced on the radio that King George V had died. After the announcement the radio only relayed solemn music interrupted by news of the King's funeral. Of course no children were allowed to play in the street and in every house curtains were drawn and remained drawn until after the funeral.

We now had a new king, King Edward VIII and I found the quick succession a bit odd but more upset was to follow because of the new king's association with a Mrs Simpson. We children didn't really understand what it was all about but we quickly learned and sang rude songs about her.

The Coronation had been set for May 12th 1937 but, as everyone knows, Edward abdicated in December 1936 and his brother George VI became king. The Coronation date was still the same but new souvenirs were hurriedly made, printed with the pictures of our new King and his Queen, Elizabeth.

Lincoln Road together with Sharman Road again held a street party, and once more, there was a great celebration.

Many articles were published about the King and Queen together with their young daughters Elizabeth and Margaret Rose. They were always dressed in matching outfits and my mother liked their coats and straw bonnets so much that she bought me an identical outfit that she saw during a visit to London.

Another outfit that was bought for me, possibly from London, was a turquoise coloured dress. It had frills all round from the waist to the hem and was in a flimsy material – very dressy.

My 'Cow pat' dress. With Papa, Nan Ives & Aunt Nora

One day we were going out for a visit. Mum went first, leaving me dressed in my finery with Dad who had strict instructions not to let me get my dress dirty. For some reason there was a long wait before Dad and I were to leave home and I got round him to let me go out until it was time to leave.

I went out to the six fields for a stroll in the sun and a calamity happened. I slipped over and landed in a very wet cow pat and got it all down the front of my dress. I ran home to Dad in a panic and he tried to clean me up in vain. There was no alternative but to take my dress off. He was laughing at me because I was pleading for the dress not to be taken over my head and I was crying and retching.

Of course he had to find another outfit for me and I have a blank in my memory about our reception when we joined Mum.

Chapter Three

Playtime

There are many happy memories of more day to day events. Dad used to take me with him regularly to the market on Saturday evenings and we came back laden with fruit and vegetables which, as I now realise, were being sold off cheaply by the traders. This was obviously a money saving exercise and some of the fruit was damaged or over-ripe but we ate and enjoyed it although I had to be persuaded that black bananas were better for me than nice white ones! He also bought a lot of boiled sweets, pear drops, clove flavoured fish shapes and aniseed balls together with licorice goodies, like shoe laces and a flat coil of liquorice with a boiled sweet tucked in the middle. Sometimes we got a bag of liquorice allsorts. I don't know if the sweets were being sold off cheaply too but it was a lovely treat to go home sucking a fish shape and seeing who could make it last longest. Dad was always partial to boiled sweets so these were probably his treat too.

In my early days I can remember travelling by tram, not all that often as we mostly walked everywhere. When we did go on the tram I used to love to go on the top deck, part of which was open aired. Mum preferred to go downstairs under cover so it was Dad who went upstairs with me. The backs of the tram seats were set in grooves so you could slide them in position so as to sit facing in your chosen direction. My favourite seat was the very front one, facing the front of course, although sometimes it was fun to switch the seat round to gaze at the other passengers. Dad was an electrician at the 'Tram Sheds' where he had started out as a driver. As Lincoln Road was at the rear of the Depot, the sheds and trams, later the buses, were almost part of my playground. Sometimes Dad took me into the sheds and even when the trams were discontinued I was allowed to play on one of those left in retirement, officially only when he was with me but I have to confess that when I was a bit older and played out in the street, my friends and I would sneak in and play on the buses. We frequently dared each other to run through the sheds from Lincoln Road to St James Main Road and back again. I wasn't very worried by that as I always had the excuse that I was looking for Dad if I was caught but another dare was to go down into the inspection pits, especially if a bus was over it, and as well as finding that a bit scary, I was very worried about getting oil on my clothes and facing the wrath of my mother, who never did know what I got up to! The sheds had metal roller doors leading out to Lincoln Road which were left open during the day but when we knew it was time for a workman to come and let them down we would hide on a bus and, yet another dare, see who would stay under cover the longest. I got a few skinned heels from staying until the last minute and dashing out to squeeze under the descending doors. It was fun and the workmen usually took it in good part. We also used the sheds, as well as the yard in games of hide and seek, the yard especially gave us some good hiding places but very dangerous too although we didn't think about that then. Old bus tyres were stored there, some put into huge piles and others stacked up, one upon the other, forming tall towers. It was quite easy to climb up the outside of a tower and then, once inside, clamber down to the bottom. It was a wonder we didn't get hurt as the towers used to wobble alarmingly and I suppose it wouldn't have taken too much to have made them collapse on top of us. Again, needless to say, Mum never knew what we were up to.

Our part of Lincoln Road was a cul-de-sac and, with the absence of traffic in those days, was a safe area to play in. We were a fairly large group of children and enjoyed many games. One favourite was What's the time Mr Wolf? in which one child was appointed Mr Wolf and stood, face to a wall, with the rest at a distance. They then advanced, calling at intervals 'What's the time Mr Wolf? and freezing when the wolf turned to answer with various times but when the wolf judged they were near enough to catch, the answer would be DINNER TIME and the wolf would then chase and try to catch one of the crowd. If successful the child caught would become the next wolf but if the wolf had misjudged and couldn't catch anyone he would have to start again. A similar game was 'Statues' where, again, one child would stand as before with the others trying to sneak up to him/her. The child would turn quickly at intervals, whereupon the rest had to instantly freeze and remain in the same position and if they wobbled or lost their position in any way they were 'out'. This continued until one managed to reach the wall or until all were 'out'. There were various 'counting out' rhymes to decide who was to be wolf or otherwise 'on' and the one we mostly used was:-

Eeny meeny miny mo
Catch a nigger by the toe
If he squeals
let him go
Eeny meeny miny mo.

Not one that would be used nowadays! Another favourite was,

Ip ip do
The cat's got the flu
Mother's got the chicken pox
And out goes you.

There were ball games, some played solo but mostly in groups, chasing games and of course, hopscotch and rounders - we were never at a loss to amuse ourselves and never bored. Skipping games were very popular too with many rhymes to go with them and if there were only two of us out to play we could always play clapping games, again with rhymes to chant.

The clapping games were always played by girls and they would face each other, clap their own hands together on the first word, right hands with each other on the second, their own hands together on the third, and with succeeding words their left hands with each other, their own hands together, and both hands with each other. They immediately restart the sequence, saying the rhyme faster and faster until one gets it wrong. A favourite rhyme was:-

My mother said
I never should
Play with the gypsies
In the wood
If I did
She would say
Naughty little girl
To disobey
Disobey
Disobey
Naughty little girl
To disobey.
Another was:-
Pease porridge hot
Pease porridge cold
Pease porridge in the pot
Nine days old
Some like it hot
Some like it cold
Some like it in the pot
Nine days old.

There were many other games - chasing, skipping and various ball games usually played against a wall. There was a very convenient wall at the house on the corner of Lincoln and Sharman Road but as our ball caused thumping noises inside the house we were often asked to go and play somewhere else. At the time we all thought this was extremely unfair!

Another game, always played by a line of girls, was 'The Big Ship Sails Through The Alley-alley-oo' which was started by one girl standing sideways to the wall with her arm forming an archway. The line then had to pass through the arch, holding hands until the girls finished up with arms crossed and linked, whereupon the first girl came away from the wall to link up with the last girl through the arch, to form a circle. While this pattern was formed everyone was singing

The big ship sails through the Alley-alley-oo
The Alley-alley-oo
The Alley-alley-oo
The big ship sails through the Alley-alley oo
On the first day of September.

Once the circle was formed the tempo of the singing was quickened, lifting and dropping the arms, until, on the last word, everyone let go.

We went through various 'crazes', such as bowling hoops, most of us had wooden ones and bowled with our hands, careering at break-neck speed up and down our part of Lincoln Road. Another time it would be spinning tops. There were two types of top that we had, one was a conical shape with a metal pin at the base and the other, called a 'window breaker', was shaped with a thick circular top and a small tubular base, again with the pin base. They could either be started to spin by a twist of the hands or by wrapping the whip round it and quickly pulling it away. Of course, once it started spinning there was keen competition to see who could keep it going the longest by flicking the top with the whip. It was possible to make them fly by whipping harder, so that the thong wrapped itself round the top, and then tossing it away as it unwound. This was easier to do with the 'window-breaker' and I suppose this is how it got its name as there was no control on direction of flight. However I never actually saw any windows broken.

There were several occasions during the year when we would all gather together to sing.

The first was Good Friday when we would go round singing

Hot cross buns, hot cross buns
One-a-penny, two-a-penny, hot cross buns
If you have no daughters, give them to your sons
One-a-penny, two-a-penny, hot cross buns.

On May 1st we girls decorated a wicker wash basket with lots of wild flowers and ribbons, put a similarly dressed doll in the middle and went from house to house to sing a Maytime song. Each group tried to outdo each other for the prettiest decorations but we all were lucky enough to be given pennies.

Of course during the days before November 5th we would make and dress a Guy, put it in a pram and take it round. As we got to each house we sang

Guy Fawkes Guy, hit him in the eye
Hang him on a lamp-post and there let him die.

Again the different groups were in competition and again the householders were generous.

The last occasion in the year was Christmas and a week or more before, not too long though, groups would go round singing carols but we only got our pennies if we sang the carol right through to the end.

In the spring we would fill our jam jars with frogs spawn from the river to bring home to watch the eggs change to tadpoles and hope to see them finally develop into frogs. Mine never reached that stage, they would grow their back legs and sometimes even their front ones but would then die one by one to my intense disappointment. No one ever told me what I did wrong. Later in the year we would take our 'bandy nets' and fish for sticklebacks but these too always came to a sad end and I would find them floating upside down in the jar. In my time I must have killed hundreds of tadpoles and small fish. My baby brother Brian did his share of thinning their numbers one memorable time when he was a toddler. I had left a jar of frogs spawn outside the back door and came back to find him taking out handfuls and eating it! Mum was horrified and worried in case it harmed him (it didn't), and I was horrified at losing the spawn. Mum tipped the rest down the drain which seemed a bit unfair to me.

Brian was into mischief another time. We had a triangular fire guard with a top that could be opened to put more coal on the fire. Mum had a habit of airing small washed items on the top of the closed guard. Brian had obviously watched her doing this and one day he opened the top and was caught feeding the fire with the clothes. Luckily the burning clothes stayed inside the guard.

During the summer we quite often left the street to play in the fields, which were part of the Six Fields, then adjacent to our part of Lincoln Road and reached by a 'jitty' between the side of Mrs T's house and the Northampton Transport Corporation land. Here we would play at houses, marking out the various rooms with stones and concocting story-lines usually involving sending the boys out to work and preparing 'meals' for them to come home to. We would gather large dock leaves to serve as plates, small stones would become potatoes, all sorts of berries and seeds would be vegetables and a sort of clover with pretty little yellow flowers (called 'eggs and bacon') would be our salad. The boys would come home from 'work' and we would all enjoy our imaginary meal. It is surprising now, how much time we devoted to this sort of game.

The older ones of our group were sometimes allowed to sleep out overnight in tents in the fields, much to the envy of the rest of us. We were judged, by our mothers', too young for such a thing. The closest we got to it was to be allowed to help put up the tent! On one occasion I was quite happy to be helping and when Mary T asked me to hold part of the tent, I trustingly took hold of it only to find to my horror, that it was a part that had been accidentally dragged through a very wet cow pat. It took a long time for me to trust her again!

Again it was only the older ones that were allowed to swim in the river across the fields, using an overhanging tree branch as a diving board. The younger group were really envious of this pastime, especially on hot days, but we never dreamed of disobeying the ban. I'm not sure if it was because we were particularly good or if it was that we knew we would get a walloping if we were caught, plus a ban on playing out. In any case we only got as far as dangling our feet in the water.

I seemed to spend most of my summers dressed in sun dresses but one day I decided that Geoff's shorts were much more practical for play in the fields. I went back home intending to borrow a pair but Mum caught me in the bathroom just as I was changing into them and soon made me get back into my dress.

The fields were always lush with buttercups, big ox eye daisies, cowslips, all sorts of lovely meadow flowers and I enjoyed picking huge bunches to bring home to Mum but I quickly learnt not to pick any May blossom for her. The first time I tried to give her a bunch of it she wouldn't have it in the house and absolutely forbade me to pick any in the future. She firmly believed it was very unlucky. The only other flower I avoided was the poppy as it was the belief of us all that if you sniffed at a poppy long enough you would fall asleep and never wake up again. Goodness knows how that story started but I believed it implicitly, after all, even a small sniff was enough to give me a headache so it must have been true!

St James, as well as other low lying parts of Northampton, suffered regular flooding and we children found it fascinating. Our playground of the Six Fields disappeared under the water so we would don our Wellingtons to see how far in we could paddle. Unfortunately, on one occasion, I completely forgot there was a ditch at the end of the field and quite suddenly I was into deep water which spilled over into my Wellingtons and wet the bottoms of my clothes. I managed to keep my balance in spite of the sudden plunge so at least I was spared a complete soaking. Needless to say, all the others in the group thought it was very funny, unfortunately my mother didn't share their amusement!

It was fun for us but not for the unfortunate folk who had their houses flooded. In later years I had a friend who lived in a road adjacent to the river and she showed me the permanent high water mark in the downstairs rooms of her home. The family had to move into the upstairs rooms until the muddy, smelly waters subsided which sometimes took days.

We played out in all weathers and during the winter frosts it was back to the street again to enjoy making long 'slides' on the paths. These, with continual use, became like highly polished glass and must have been terrible booby traps for unwary pedestrians. Although I don't recall any adult slipping on one I do remember that, occasionally, a parent would come out to sprinkle salt on the ice to melt it. We used to have great fun with a slide, forming a line to use it and then running as quickly as possible to the start again. If there was enough of us out to play it was perpetual motion. Any child who fell and broke the rhythm was in dire disgrace.

We children of Lincoln and Sharman Road always played together in groups with surprisingly few disputes and roamed the fields and the two streets freely. We were set our boundaries by our parents and stuck to them as to disobey was to lose this precious freedom for a while. Looking back now I wonder how we always knew when it was time for a meal as although none of us had watches we always managed, at the appropriate times, to be near enough to the houses to hear when a mother called from the garden or front door. Mrs T had the loudest voice so maybe we took the cue from her.

My mother was very strict about the way I spoke and no trace of the Northampton accent was allowed. She would have given me a smack if I had said something like 'I ain't gooing' instead of 'I'm not going'. This led me to have two languages, one for home and one for the street as I quickly realised that to speak to my pals in my 'home' way would label me as being 'posh' or 'stuck-up' or both!

She was also strict about Sunday observance and I was never allowed to play out in the street on Sundays and I don't think my pals were either. At least I was allowed to play with toys in the house or garden and I was horrified when my mother told me that, when she was young, she was born in 1901, she was only allowed to read special books on Sunday, appropriately called 'Sunday Annuals', and had to go to Chapel Sunday School three times each week.

One day my friend Nancy and I were the only ones out to play and I decided we ought to walk to Harlestone Firs. I didn't realise that it was three or more miles away, a long way for two small girls. It was a very hot day and at first we enjoyed walking in the sunshine but soon we began to get thirsty. When we passing a line of houses I decided to call on one to ask for a glass of water and also to ask if we had much farther to go. The lady who answered our knock on her door must have been very surprised at our request but she kindly gave us a drink and told us that we still had a long way to walk to the Firs. In fact it must have been about a mile still to go but we had no idea of the distance. We thanked her and walked on but after a few yards we thought that perhaps we had gone far enough so we turned round and made our way back home. I don't know how long we were away but our parents hadn't even missed us. As we hadn't told them where we were going they must have thought we were playing near to home. I'm sure that Mum would have forbidden us to go so far but she never knew our plan to walk to Harlestone Firs!

Groups of friends went for other walks nearer home. Upton was one place via Duston Mill but a place we all loved was Hunsbury Hill where we would picnic on the grassy mounds that were over the long railway tunnel underneath. We never got tired of listening, with our ears to the ground, for a train coming and then watching the smoke coming out of the brick chimneys that were built at intervals along the line.

Chapter Four

Local Family Visits

My Nan Britten had a sweet shop in the Main Road near to Mill Road and, of course, I really enjoyed visiting her to 'help' in the shop. Again I was allowed to go on my own and trusted to cross the Main Road. Nan would always find a little job for me to do but my absolute favourite was breaking up the slab toffee. It was an oblong shaped slab in a metal tray and came with a special little hammer to break up the toffee, ready to weigh out and serve in conical bags for small amounts and rectangular ones for larger. If any of the pieces I broke were too small to serve I was allowed to eat them. Needless to say quite a few pieces found their way into my mouth and as well as that, I only had to gaze longingly at a sweet and say how nice it looked for Nan to pop that too into my mouth. I found out many years later that Mum had to ask Nan not to give in to me as when I got home from a visit to her, I couldn't eat my meal but Nan was so soft hearted that she still gave me the sweets but let me put them in a bag to take home. She had to give up the shop in the end as she let too many of her customers have credit and virtually gave away her profits. There were two more sweet shops quite near to her, one shabby little one next to Facer's cycle shop and another, better class one, the other side of

Ambush Street. There was Handley's the tobacconist and Hardwick's, a baker/grocer who also stocked sweets which were the next two shops across the little alley between Nan's shop and Hardwick's so, all in all, she had a lot of competition and could ill afford to be so generous. Naturally, I was blissfully unaware of all this and was just so sorry for wrong reasons when Nan left the shop.

Sunday morning was an interesting time to visit Nan for although all the shops were shut, the bakery was always doing a roaring trade. Ladies would come in a steady stream to the side door in the alley dividing Nan's shop from the bakery, bringing their roasting tins containing their meat and Yorkshire pudding for Mr Hardwick to cook in his ovens. At dinner time, it was always dinner not lunch then, they would all come back to collect them and carry away delicious looking roasts, surrounded by perfectly puffed up Yorkshires puddings. The tins must have been marked in some way or else Mr Hardwick knew all his customers extremely well as I never heard of any one given the wrong dish. The smell in that alley on Sunday mornings was just wonderful.

Further along this same alley, which I think was called Whitford Terrace, it opened up to reveal a small row of tiny terraced houses each with a small yard in front. It all looked very poverty stricken but I never got to know much about the people who lived there as I was not allowed to go near them. Sometimes I would venture to the end of the alley and peer round the corner at the houses as they fascinated me, partly because it was forbidden territory I suppose. Along the Main Road, just past Doddridge Chapel, there were three or four similar houses and these too were occupied by poor people who seemed to have a lot of children. The children of our 'gang' were all warned not to play with them as they were supposed to have all sorts of diseases, scabies, impetigo etc., but they didn't come over to our territory much anyway as the Main Road was a barrier. I remember one sad looking little boy who had a very blue skin but we didn't know then that it was because of a heart problem, and if he did appear in our streets some of the boys made fun of his appearance. I cringe now to think of that and I'm glad I didn't join in, Mum had told me not to tease him as the child was not very well. I suppose he didn't live all that long.

Almost every Saturday we visited my other grand parents, Nan and Papa Ives, for tea and sometimes, supper too. The teas were a scaled down version of the Christmas spread and made up for the boredom of having to listen to the 'grown-ups' chatter, especially as children were very much seen but not heard in those days. Usually we could only speak if spoken to!

I was always sent to Tarpley's dairy, just over the road from Nan's, to buy fresh cream for the tinned fruit and that was an errand I really enjoyed. It was always so cool and fresh smelling in the shop which had a marble counter and tiled walls - the tiles were patterned with dairy themes. On hot days I never used to mind how long it took before someone came to serve me as, although I was usually the only one there, for some reason or other, I was still kept waiting. Eventually though Mrs Tarpley would appear from behind the curtained door and I would hand over my jug to be filled. She had different sized shiny measures and would dip one of them into the churn and then carefully pour the cream into the jug without spilling a drop. Occasionally I had to buy milk too so I had to be very careful carrying two jugs back over the road.

Another regular treat was a plate of fancy cakes which Nan bought from Steads bakery in Wellingborough Road and I was always careful to leave enough room to eat one of these. We children were allowed first choice of cakes and Geoff often used to tease me. He would politely offer the plate, note which cake I favoured and then, just as I reached for it, he would quickly turn the plate round so that I couldn't take it. I would fall for it every time!

The only cake I didn't like was home made seed cake. I hated the taste of the carroway seeds which seemed to linger in the mouth for a long time.

If we stayed for supper I was sent to Wilford's, the outdoor beer shop, in Whitworth Road, to get a jug of beer for the men. Nan had a special jug for this and I would carry it to the shop, rehearsing in my head what I had to ask for. Mr Wilford had (I think) three tapped barrels behind the counter and filled my jug from one of them, right to the top with a good head of froth. It was quite a job to carry it back to Nan's. I was always fascinated by the serving of the beer but I didn't much like the smell. Certainly I was never tempted to try any on the way back.

Supper took place as soon as I arrived so that the beer didn't go flat and Nan usually served cheese, home-made pickles with tomatoes and cress together with lots of lovely crusty bread.

The front room wasn't used much apart from Christmas when, after the meal the adults always played whist in there. The room had a view straight down the Avenue opposite to the Wellingborough Road at the bottom and Nan sometimes liked to sit on one of the chairs, either side of an aspidistra, to enjoy the comings and goings of folk, especially her neighbours.

I loved Nan's house, always so tidy and smelling of polish. She left school when she was only 13 years old and went into service so she knew everything about keeping house.

In the front room she had a lovely Grandmother clock and in the living/dining room there was a wall clock. Both had beautiful chimes which sounded really nice on the hours and quarters.

The living room was more lived in and the large table and chairs and two easy chairs either side of the fireplace plus a sideboard didn't leave much room. The legs and the stretcher bars underneath the table were covered with corrugated cardboard to guard from childrens' scrapes and we weren't allowed to put our feet inside the tiled surround of the fireplace but even these restrictions didn't detract from my enjoyment of visiting Nan and Papa.

The wireless in one corner stood on a table with books on the shelves underneath. One of those books was a medical dictionary which, from quite a young age, I liked to look at. I'm surprised now that I wasn't told to put it away as the illustrations were quite graphic. Perhaps they thought I wouldn't understand them.

There were three bedrooms, two at the back and Nan and Papa's at the front and all had very comfortable feather beds on brass bedsteads.

The kitchen was the biggest room with a large table in front of a dresser.

On the opposite side was a shallow sink and in the corner was a copper for laundry, and for steaming the Christmas puddings. The water in the copper was drawn from a tap over the sink and heated by a fire underneath it.

I think Nan used to do this on the Sunday evening so that all was ready to do the wash on Monday morning.

There was a short passage beyond the kitchen which led to a toilet, very dark and in the winter very cold. A paraffin heater was used to avoid the pipes freezing.

From there the passage finished in a conservatory which housed gardening equipment and a huge heavy mangle to wring the water from the laundry. The clothes had to be rinsed and mangled several times, a process which took most of the morning. At some time during the wash a blue bag was put in which somehow made the whites brighter. Nan was a small, slightly built lady but she did all this every week. I used to help with the mangling when I stayed with her and I found it hard to get the clothes through the rollers.

The washing was hung out to dry on the line in the garden and fetched in whilst it was still damp which made it easier to iron. Nan did this on the kitchen table which was covered first by a folded blanket. When Nan changed from ironing with flat irons heated on the gas burners, she used an electric iron which she heated by taking the lamp out of the electric light and plugged in the iron. My mother used to do the same.

Also leading from the kitchen were the steps to the coal cellar. Coal was delivered through a window from the pavement at the front of the house and I was sometimes delegated to stand in the cellar to count the number of bags the coalman emptied.

Nan used to fill a scuttle and carry it up to the living room. Another heavy job but although Nan was so tiny she was also very strong and healthy. She once fell down the cellar steps and was quite badly bruised but she shrugged it off as a trivial mishap.

She lived to the age of 88 yrs and unfortunately died of cancer but before then I don't remember her ever being ill although she did take to her bed after a nasty fall on wet leaves one autumn day. My mother insisted that she came to our house so that she could be looked after but she soon recovered and went home.

I often sat on the floor in front of my much loved Papa and one of my favourite occupations was to make spills from newspaper for him to light his cigarettes.

When I was quite small I was occasionally taken to visit a very old lady, or so she seemed to me then, who lived in a terraced house in the Clare Street area. I don't know how she was related to me but everyone in the family called her Aunt 'Vene, short for the pretty name Lavinia I suppose, and if we visited on warm days we would usually find her sitting on a chair set outside her front door, as were most of her neighbours. It was all very sociable.

Some time later when Aunt Vene was a patient in St Edmunds hospital, Papa was informed by the hospital that she had died. The family was told and funeral arrangements were started.

It was close to Christmas and Uncle Frank Ives was with the Mayoral party making their Seasonal visit to the hospital. Aunt Vene spotted him and complained bitterly that no one had visited her. He was amazed to say the least at seeing her but managed to pacify her before going to inform Papa that Aunt Vene was still alive.

When enquiries started it was found that, during the cleaning of the ward, the beds had been pushed to the centre of the ward, as was usual. The patients' folders in those days were on the wall behind each bed and somehow Aunt Vene had been pushed back in front of the wrong notes. In fact it was the lady in the next bed who had died when she was in the bed in front of Aunt Vene's notes.

I wonder if that's when they started clipping patients' notes to the bottom of their beds!

There was a relative I don't remember visiting but, because I was fascinated by words and would always use a long word if I could, Dad christened me 'Aunt Ginnie', as she always did the same.

There was another visit of which I have a faint memory. It was to another of the Ives clan, Christopher, his wife Eva and their son Bob. Their bungalow was in the middle of a field, or so it seemed to me. The only part of the visit I clearly remember is Geoff driving Bob and I round the field in our car. Geoff was only about 12 yrs old but we weren't worried and thought it was great fun. When Mum and Dad realised what we were doing they were not amused and our ride came to an abrupt halt.

Uncle Chris was a Spiritualist and firmly believed in contacting folk after their death. When I was older and they lived in Northampton I used to visit them. He had a wonderful painting which he had done, of a Red Indian in full feathered head dress and I was told that this was a painting of his 'Guide' to the after world. If a door opened for no apparent reason in his or any other house he would solemnly say "Welcome whoever you are". I was always a bit of a giggler and Mum used to tell me not to dare laugh if he ever said it in front of us – which he did.

I used to visit Nan Britten quite often but Mum, Dad and Geoff didn't. She used to come to see us but never seemed to be welcomed which was a shame. She now lived in a flat in Kingsthorpe Hollow and when I visited she always had tea and cake on offer. I liked to encourage her to talk about my Grandfather who was the Town Hall Keeper. He died in office in 1922 so of course I never knew him but I liked to hear about him. She still had his uniform and kept it, wrapped in tissue paper, in a drawer. It was very colourful with red trousers and a coat with red trimmings. He used to wear a silver badge of office on his sleeve but of course she couldn't keep that. A top hat went with the uniform but I never saw that either. However she had a lovely coloured painting of him in full uniform which now hangs in our house.

Although Nan was quite sprightly she always complained to us of various ills which got her no sympathy at all from Mum and Dad especially as we often saw her walking briskly but starting to limp or stagger when she got nearer our house. She had already told us that she would join a queue for off the ration goods and then start to stagger. Sympathetic shoppers would then pass her to the top of the queue. She would chuckle wickedly as she told us but I have to say, she never gained the items for herself, she passed them on to us.

I was the only one at home one day when she came and she complained to me that her head was getting bigger and she couldn't get her hat on very well. I could see that she was right and made sympathetic conversation whilst I made her some tea.

Mum and Dad arrived after she left and said 'What was wrong with her this time?' When I told them they couldn't stop laughing even though I told them it seemed to be true. I don't know how long it was after this that she got worse and eventually she was diagnosed with Paget's Disease.

Mum wanted to have her to our house so that she could nurse her but was urged not to by the doctor as the bone deformity of her skull would eventually damage the brain. When that happened Nan would probably become violent and Mum wouldn't be able to cope.

Because of this possibility Nan had to go into a nursing home and died soon after.

Nan had relatives living in a poor part of Northampton and she badly wanted me to visit them. Mum and Dad didn't want me to go but I felt I couldn't disappoint Nan. I made several visits but it was never easy. They were extremely surprised when I turned up on their doorstep and seemed very uneasy in my company. At one point they said that I supposed they weren't good enough for me to visit them.

The family consisted of Aunt Rose and Uncle Reg and their three adult children. I liked the eldest girl best as she belonged to St John's Ambulance Brigade and said she would help me to join. Unfortunately it never happened. Their only son was young Reg and it was him who said they weren't good enough and teased me about it. The other daughter, Rosie, suffered from what Mum called creeping paralysis. She was very physically disabled but in those days she was labelled a cripple.

Because of their discomfort my visits dwindled and eventually I stopped going. I never got to know much about them and although I knew their surname was Miller. I didn't know if they were aunt and uncle.

Chapter Five

Swimming

W e did a lot of swimming in our family and I can barely remember a time when I was unable to swim.

My very first memories were of going to a field that had a small river running through it, belonging to, I believe, Clifford Mill, near Cogenhoe. We and various members of our family used to spend many happy hours there together with our neighbours, Mr. and Mrs Allen (Nell and Ted) and their lodgers, Mr and Mrs Partridge. We always took a picnic with us and stayed there until dusk. I can't remember how we got there but I believe that Dad had a motor cycle and sidecar at that time and he probably ferried us a few at a time. I actually couldn't swim when we first went there so I was probably only about four but I soon realised that to be unable to swim was to miss out on a lot of the fun so I quickly took my first strokes.

My strongest memories are of a swimming pool which was an open air bathing pool made from part of the river Nene and heated by the electricity cooling towers on the opposite side. I remember that it was very old fashioned and men and women were strictly segregated. There were two entrances, one for the women and girls to pay and go through a turnstile at one end, and at the far end for the men and boys to do likewise. Once inside the sexes filtered off to their own changing areas, again strictly segregated. At the kiosk at the entrance to the changing cubicles you were given a numbered metal box and a rubber band with a matching number. Then you went to a cubicle to change, put your clothes in the box and handed it to the lady in the kiosk, keeping the rubber band (usually worn on the wrist or ankle) to hand in when you wanted to get your clothes back. Once changed of course everyone was free to mix but the pool attendants made sure that no male was allowed to loiter near the women's changing area. The attendants were very strict, in this respect as well as with behaviour in and around the pool. Absolutely no bad behaviour was allowed and if any was spotted it was dealt with – anyone larking about too much in the water was told to get out. No one argued! On the opposite side of the pool was a large grass area, used for games, picnicking or just sun bathing – deck chairs were available for hire and there was also a refreshment kiosk.

The pool was large with an area at the shallow end for children and non swimmers separated by a floating barrier from the larger expanse marked 'Swimmers Only'. It was quite wide too and had posts in the middle marked to tell you the depth of water which were handy to grab hold of if you felt need of a rest. These posts were to loom large in my memory as one day Dad decided I could swim well enough to attempt to swim the width of the pool, so off I set with him swimming at my side. We reached the middle and he decided to let me hold on to a post to have a break. Fine, except when he wanted me to swim away, I lost my nerve and wouldn't let go again! I clung like a limpet with my arms and legs tightly round the post and he tried coaxing, scolding, even trying to drag me away to no avail. It wasn't until he told me that the pool attendants were about to dive in to get me, and I saw he was telling the truth, that I finally plucked up courage and let go to complete the width. He made me swim back again, but this time in one go, just to prove to me that I was able to do it.

During summer holidays and weekends a huge party of us would make for Midsummer Meadow, affectionately known as 'Middy'. With our neighbours and relatives we would set out from Lincoln Road, carrying our costumes and towels plus our picnic, walking along St James Main Road to just opposite Park Road where we would then cross Foot Meadow, under the railway arches, past the gas works and cross Victoria Promenade into Becket's Park, which was then known as Cow Meadow. We would usually stop at Becket's Well to fill bottles with the ice cold spring water flowing there. After walking through the park and finally across Midsummer Meadow we were more than ready for a swim. Sometimes we got there before they opened and had to wait impatiently in our separate queues so we were always glad if the queues were not too long. We always tried to get there early so that we could get a good place on the grass area where we would soon be joined by the rest of the group, family and friends, eventually numbering about sixteen adults and half a dozen children. The picnics were all put together and we had a good feast and the only part I didn't like was tea from a vacuum flask! We younger ones usually had Tizer or Corona (the latter was delivered at home, once a week, in crates of four bottles with a choice of flavours) and of course, the spring water from Becket's Well. The big draw back of all this feasting and drinking was that we weren't allowed to swim afterwards for an hour – we children were told, and we believed it, that we would sink straight to the bottom if we went in too soon. The time was passed with playing games, usually rounders and French cricket. The men, for some strange reason, would often form pyramids with the strongest at the bottom and the lightest, usually my brother Geoff, at the top.

I would long to join in this but was never allowed to, possibly because they eventually lost balance and collapsed in a heap!

Swimming antics

When the prescribed hour was up we all went off for more swimming. Most of the group were swimmers, in fact Nan Ives took her first strokes there. She was nearly sixty years old and we were all so thrilled for her. At the other end of the age scale was my baby brother, Brian. He used to love every minute of the times we spent at the pool and, right from babyhood, loved to be taken into the water. When he was about 18 months old he gave everyone a bit of a fright. He was at the edge of the pool and having great fun jumping in to be caught by Papa. After many such jumps he was being shepherded back to our 'pitch' when he must have decided he wanted one more jump so, quick as a flash, he turned, ran back to the edge and leapt into the water. By this time Papa had started to swim away and there was no one there to catch him. He went straight down to the bottom! Lots of people shouted and came to help but Papa moved quicker than he had ever done before and got to him first. He grabbed Brian and brought him to the surface blinking and spluttering and looking extremely surprised. Luckily he thought it was all part of the game and once he got his breath back, was laughing and asking for more. It took the rest of us a little longer to start laughing with him.

I could swim well enough but had a great deal of trouble learning to dive. Dad and the others would spend time with me making me take up the right stance but always, at the very last minute, I would jump! I would try and try on my own but could never do it until one day, when I was again teetering on the edge, a boy ran by, gave me a push, and in I went – head first. From then on there was no stopping me and I soon graduated to diving from the diving boards at the end of the pool. The only slight problem was that I always went in like a stone and it didn't matter how deep the pool was, I always went straight to the bottom. It wasn't until many years later when I swam for my high school, that I was taught a racing dive and that cured it. Alas, my fun diving was over after a few years, spoilt by a thoughtless prank. A group of us were testing ourselves to see who could stay under the water the longest and having a great time outdoing each other. After several rounds it was my turn again and I stayed under until I thought I would burst but as I started to surface one of the boys put his hands on the top of my head and stopped me. I kicked and punched him in complete panic and he had to let me surface, but the damage was done and, to this day, I have always avoided diving. In fact I can't bear anything over my face that might stop me from breathing, as it brings on that same feeling of panic.

When closing time came the attendants blew whistles to clear the pool but they had to blow many times as, part of the fun was to see who could be the last one in the water. By the time we had reclaimed our clothes the changing cubicles were all in use so, quite often, some of us had to go back over to the grass and change behind towels held by willing members of our group.

We visited other pools but they were never so much fun as Middy Meadow. I remember Billing Aquadrome as just a swimming pool and in those days we always said we were going over to Mackaness'es. They owned the nearby gravel pits and I believe the pool originated from a disused pit. However the bottom was still gravelled and seemed to shift. I didn't really like to swim there at all as you could, unknowingly, get out of your depth. A bit disconcerting when you tried to stand and went under the water instead!

I can't remember how we got over to Billing but it was probably the same way we reached Overstone Solarium. My father seemed to have use of a car from time to time and on these occasions he would ferry us as he did with the motor cycle and side car on our trips to Clifford Mill. He would fill the car and drive off leaving the rest of us to start walking. After dropping off the first load he would drive back, meet us along the road and take a second load, repeating this until we were all at our destination. We children were always the last to be picked up so we had quite a long way to walk. The road down Ecton Lane to Wellingborough Road seemed extremely long on a hot summer evening when our legs were tired from all the swimming and playing but we never cheated by taking a rest. In any case Dad knew exactly where we should be when it was finally our turn to climb into the car.

The pool at the Solarium was quite pretty, set in parkland, but the water was icy cold, even on a very hot day. I well remember Papa diving in for the first time when the shock of the cold water actually took his breath away. I shall never forget the look of his face when he surfaced, gasping for air. In the family it was considered 'sissy' to hesitate or dither about going into the water so as soon as we were able, we were expected to dive or jump in. However at Overstone, I usually used to risk scorn and would get in via the steps, ducking under when I was about waist deep.

There was one more swimming place I occasionally used but only with friends. As far as I remember, my parents never went there. It was near the junction of St Andrew's Road and Spencer Bridge Road, again a pool annexed from the river. It was always called Paddy's Meadow but I don't know if it had an official name. I didn't go there very often as it wasn't very attractive and quite often it was dirty too. When one day, as I was swimming and some disgusting human waste floated past my nose, I got out of the pool and never went there again.

When the indoor swimming baths were opened in 1936 at the Mounts, we were able to swim in all seasons. The baths were promptly christened the 'New Baths' and to this day the name is used by old Northamptonians. It was considered very luxurious and, after a swim, it was pleasant to buy a doughnut with a drink from the snack bar, then going up to the balcony to enjoy them while watching the other swimmers. There were other facilities as well as the pool although I have never used any of them. You could indulge in a Turkish bath and/or have a massage – no sleazy connotations then!

From school we had swimming lessons at Barry Road school baths. It was very basic with just the pool, no spring boards. Diving, from the side only and with permission from the attendant There were cubicles, each with a waterproof curtain. Changing wasn't easy as there was barely room to turn round.

Barry Road Baths

We were able to take our distance length tests there and I qualified for my 60 yards certificate. It was there too that I was taught the racing dive ready for competing in swimming galas held at the Mounts pool.

I remember a lady, Lil Gambel but I don't remember her role there. I think she was a life saver and, possibly, a swimming instructor too. She was very strict and would allow no playing about in the water. She was well known and respected in the town. I have seen photos of the pool at Barry Road taken in the early 1900s and it still looked exactly the same when our classes went. Many Northampton children were taught to swim there and remember it with a certain amount of affection.

Chapter Six

More Shops

Shops always fascinated me, possibly because of Nan Britten's sweet shop and also that of my Aunt Florrie, my favourite great aunt and Uncle Frank Burgess. Uncle Frank was blind in one eye and, like many men with that handicap, was taught the art of piano tuning which led him to owning a shop to sell pianos. I always loved to visit them although, I have to admit, it was Aunt Florrie's company I most enjoyed as Uncle Frank never had much to say and was quite mean. He used to sit in his chair, smoking a foul smelling pipe, and in the winter we huddled over a fire made with just one lump of coal, which he turned at intervals to even the burning. There was never a cheerful flame, just a dull red smouldering glow on one side of the piece of coal. However Aunt Florrie used to make me my favourite cherry cake and generally spoiled me. They had no children of their own.

Their shop was in Wellingborough Road between Abington Square and St Edmunds hospital, quite a narrow road in those days but all the shops along that side of the road were demolished when the road was widened in the 1960's. There was a large plate glass window to the front of the shop showing the pianos tastefully arranged in rows in the show room.

A glazed door was at the side of the window and when opened it rang a little bell, which brought Uncle Frank out from behind a chenille curtain covering the door to the living room at the back of the property. That room was quite small and had yet another curtain covered door which opened on to a narrow twisting staircase leading to a bedroom. I realise now that this room was very 'Victorian' and I used to love to stand in there, listening to the sound of the traffic in the road outside and, I suppose, just soaking up the atmosphere. The show room was the largest room of the property and I was often allowed to dust the pianos, totally unnecessary as everything was immaculate, when I would take the opportunity to play on the keys. I was absolutely forbidden to go in if Uncle Frank had a customer but I used to listen from behind the curtain as he played a piano to demonstrate the tone.

Aunt Florrie was a lovely person and seemed very popular with the other shopkeepers, especially the Pells next door who were house furnishers. The next shop, on the corner of Cleveland Road was Mence Smith's the hardware dealers, a branch of the bigger shop on Mercers Row in town centre. When I visited Aunt Florrie it was my custom to put my head round the doors of her neighbours to call 'Hello' - their doors were always left open so that people could go in and browse.

Two doors up towards St Edmunds Hospital was a ladies hairdresser, Whymants, and it was there that I was taken to have my hair permed for the very first time. I must have been about seven years old and my Uncle George, Mum's only brother, was getting married to Auntie Doll. I was to be one of the bridesmaids and it was obviously thought that I would look prettier with curly hair so, feeling extremely apprehensive, I was put into the hands of Jack Whymant. My hair was treated with an evil smelling solution, wound onto metal curlers after which each curler was clamped with another contraption. These were attached by leads to a stand which in turn was plugged into the electricity supply. The curlers and the attachments were very heavy but it was necessary to sit there until the perm 'took'. I don't know how long this was but, to me, it seemed as if it was for ever and I daren't move at all in fact the whole process was quite terrifying. I can't remember what came next but I suppose a neutralising operation took place and eventually Aunt Florrie collected me transformed into a curly headed little girl. I rather think Shirley Temple had something to answer for! Everyone seemed happy with the result until the next day when, horror of horrors, amongst all those curls one piece of hair stuck out, straight as it ever was - one curl hadn't taken! I was taken back to the hairdresser who, with very bad grace, went through the whole process again but with only the one piece of hair. He was extremely grumpy throughout and I sat there feeling it was all my fault.

My hair was usually attended to at a barbers shop opposite St James Church, always referred to by the locals as 'Patsy Burke's'. I was sent there to have fringe and bobbed hair trimmed but I think it was a shop mainly for men. I don't know if Mum made an appointment but I always had to wait my turn. The shop had a counter and cash till at the front of the shop behind which was the hairdressing and barber's department. I would take my place on one of the chairs facing the hairdressers at work and would watch other customers being attended to. I think the thing that most fascinated me was the 'singeing'. After the hair was cut and clipped the barber would light a taper from the gas jet and singe the hair at the back of the neck, apparently to seal the hairs. It looked a horrendous process and the smell of scorched hair was not very pleasant either, but contrary to my fears, no-one ever lost all their hair to the flame.

When my turn came I was lifted into the chair, enveloped in a huge overall and then had to follow instructions - look up, look down etc - while the scissors were applied. The worst bit was having my fringe trimmed as I hated seeing the scissors flash in front of my face and even though I blinked hard stray hairs always seemed to find their way into my eyes. The clippers weren't very nice as sometimes hair got caught in the blades to give a painful tug when the hairdresser moved on too quickly. I was always glad to escape from the chair in spite of usually feeling quite chilly round my neck after my hair cut. I used to pay at the counter and it was there that I once got a free jig saw puzzle of 'Bubbles' from the picture by Millais. I believe it was given away with the purchase of Colgate tooth paste but however I got it, I loved it.

There were two other popular hairdressers in St James Main Road,

Burmans and Sam Malin. Sam Malin was the one most favoured by my father but as Burman's was a bit nearer I think he also went there.

Our local shop was Mrs Robinson's, on the corner of Lincoln and Sharman Road which was where Mum got her groceries and I spent my Saturday pennies on sweets. I was usually sent to the shop to get bread and once got into serious trouble when I arrived home with a warm loaf minus a crust. The delicious smell of the freshly baked bread was too much for me and I thought Mum wouldn't notice if I broke off a small piece to taste. Unfortunately once I'd done that I wanted more and by the time I got home the whole of one end of the loaf had vanished, making it impossible to hide my greed. Mum was furious and I was in deep disgrace - I never did it again, I was much too scared of my mother's anger!

There are happier memories of the shop. The pavement outside was often a meeting place for the Sharman Road and our Lincoln Road groups, I suppose we could have been labelled as gangs but, on the whole, we were all friendly and although we had our 'home' territories we also met together on neutral ground such as the 'Six Fields' and, of course, Robinson's corner.

When I had a Saturday penny to spend I would lean with my nose pressed to the window, trying to decide what sweets to buy. The attractive display always made the decision difficult but as the prices ranged from a farthing upwards I could get at least four different sorts for my penny. One of my many favourites was a 'Sunday Dinner' selection and there was a choice of little chickens, new potatoes and green peas, all made of marzipan and looking very realistic. Mrs Robinson would put them in a little paper cone but when I got them home I would carefully arrange them on a plate from my dolls tea service. I would do this with dolly mixtures too. Other favourites were liquorice 'bootlaces' as well as the thicker strips coiled up with a brightly coloured hard sweet in the centre. Sometimes I would buy a packet of sweet cigarettes and pretend to smoke like my father but they were a bit sickly and I usually ended up regretting wasting my money on them. There were plenty of other sweets in the window, chocolate drops, coconut chips, liquorice allsorts, pontefract cakes, marzipan tea cakes (which never tasted like marzipan) and of course there were also the jars of the different sorts of boiled sweets and trays of toffee. In fact Robinson's had almost the same assortment of boiled and liquorice sweets that Dad used to buy on our visits to the Market. Other glass jars held kali, one of lemon flavour and another of bright multi coloured powder, I don't know what flavour that was supposed to be! We would buy a bagful and eat it by dipping our finger in and licking off the powder which would then fizz delightfully in the mouth. In the summer we would buy the lemon flavour and dissolve it in water to make 'lemonade', not very good but a lot cheaper than a bottle of pop. There was usually a small group of us all trying to make up our minds and we would often decide on our purchases with a promise to swap – our early version of 'Pick and Mix'! On the counter inside the shop you could pay ¼d (a farthing)or ½d (a ha'penny) for a sort of lucky dip with a shallow box containing a number of compartments, each containing a different coloured bead and all concealed by a cover of flimsy paper. For each price you were allowed a number of stabs with a metal 'stabber' to pierce the paper and release the ball. Each colour won you a different value prize, the lowest giving you perhaps just one sweet but if you were lucky enough to release a gold or silver ball you got a higher value prize and could choose between chocolate bars and extra big sherbet dips. The dips were sherbet in a triangular paper packet with a liquorice 'straw' sticking out from one corner and a tiny caramel flavoured lollipop (a dab) from another. You had a choice therefore of getting at the sherbet. I usually used the dab first and finished off the sherbet by sucking it through the liquorice. The final choice was which to eat first, the straw or the dab.

During the summer months we would wait on the corner for the Wall's ice cream man to come so that we could buy 1d Sno Fruits, Sno Creams or, if we had more money, 2d paper wrapped blocks supplied with two wafer biscuits. The Sno Fruits were long triangular water ices enclosed in thin cardboard, the Sno Creams were milky ices. They came in various fruit flavours and we would start licking at one end, gradually pushing the ice up by folding the cardboard at the other, being extremely careful not to let the very last piece tumble to the ground. The ice cream cart was a cycle with an iced carrier at the front, painted in distinctive dark blue and white.

The man would always signal his approach by ringing the bell on the cycle whilst calling out "Walls Ice Cream - Stop Me and Buy One".

Another welcome visitor to the corner was the barrel organ and we would run to our mothers' to get some money to put in his tin so that he would play some extra tunes.

Towards Christmas the Salvation Army band would tour the streets playing carols and once again Robinson's corner was a venue so it meant that all year through there was something to amuse us.

I was sent on errands to other shops further afield, a regular one was to the Co-op butcher on St James Square and very early in life I learned Mum's Divi (dividend) number, 4071. A Co-op member was issued with a number on joining and it had to be given at every purchase. The shop assistant had a special book with pink slips in it and on each transaction he entered the number, giving a copy to the customer and keeping the counterfoil in the book. At the end of the year each member would receive a dividend on the total amount spent, Divi day was always a day to look forward to. The money had to be collected from the large Co-op department store in Abington Street and I always liked to go there as, when a purchase was made the shop assistant would take your money and put into a special carrier which was sent whizzing on an overhead wire system to the cash office. In a few moments a carrier was whizzing back bringing the receipt, change, plus, of course, the little pink slip, bearing the magic number 4071.

It's amazing that even now ladies of a certain age can immediately recall their mother's Co-op divvy number.

Chapter Seven

Town Centre

My mother always went 'up' town but my Nan went 'down' so I was never quite sure which I should say, however, a walk into town was always enjoyable, we usually walked there but occasionally caught a bus back home. There was always a pause on West Bridge for me to be lifted so that I could peer over to see the trains and then it was on past the station, up Black Lion Hill to Marefair. One of the most fascinating shops in Marefair was that of the taxidermist, Geo. Bazeley. The stuffed animals in the window never failed to amaze me, they seemed so real but when I was very young I don't think I realized that they were once living creatures.

On the other side of the road was a very different sort of establishment. It was a cafe, or dining rooms as described by the painted sign on the window: The owner was Mrs Andrews. The window display consisted of sausages, mushy peas, onions and potatoes in their separate metal trays. The shop door was always open releasing an appetising smell which wafted over a large part of Marefair. I would walk slowly past, savouring the aroma as well as gazing in at the busy scene.

Gold Street had some beautiful shops and I never tired of looking at their displays. However the two shops I favoured, others were way beyond my Saturday pocket money means, were Woolworths with their slogan, nothing over 6d, and the Marks & Spencer Penny Bazaar. These were where I bought birthday and Christmas presents for the family and it was a challenge to get the most I could for my pennies. It always took me ages to decide so sometimes Mum would leave me in the store whilst she did other shopping. This gave me a lot more time to browse before parting with my cash. One year I bought a Christmas present for Papa. It was an oak barrel with a plaque on it to say the wood was from HMS Victory. I bought a pack of spills to go in it.

Woolworths was quite big and had a variety of goods on sale from three counters stretching the length of the shop. The frontage was narrow so the inside of the shop had just two aisles, again right down to the end, with stalls either side.

Marks & Spencer also had a narrow frontage but had just one counter but this was Aladdin's cave to me as they sold all sorts of little items, ornaments, combs, mirrors, note books, hair slides and all manner of nick knacks within my price range.

At the very top of Gold Street, going round the corner into the Drapery, was Boots the Chemist. I don't recall the ground floor of the shop, I suppose it was like most chemist shops, but downstairs was a large library. Mum was an avid reader and a member of Boots as well as the Public Library in Abington Street. I enjoyed browsing round the shelves while she made her choice of books to borrow.

The market was another magic place for me with the stall holders shouting above each other to sell their wares. In the centre, next to the ornamental fountain, was a man with big weighing scales and I would love to step onto the platform and watch him moving the weights and then carefully sliding the pointer along the rule on the cross bar to finish up with the correct weight. He would then write it on a ticket and hand it over for a payment of a penny or two. I enjoyed the market most after dark when the stalls were lit by their big, hissing hurricane lamps giving off the pungent smell of naphtha. As I said in an earlier chapter, towards the end of the day was the time for selling off the surplus produce and a lot of bargains were to be had. It was all very exciting.

Every year we bought poppies for Armistice Day, November 11th and on the day itself at 11 o clock everything and everyone stopped for a 2 minute silence to remember those who died in the Great War. It made a huge impression on me and it was especially striking to be in the Town Centre at that time. To be part of the mass remembrance was very moving. I'm glad that we have now reverted to a silence on that day if only one minute, to pay respect to all our war victims. During the days following the 11th, many people 'planted' their poppy in the grass near the War Memorial at the back of All Saints church and we always went to put ours there. They were special poppies, the flower mounted onto a little cross and soon they made a sea of red round the Cenotaph, the base of which was covered by the huge wreathes placed by the various dignitaries and officials of the town. It was always a special moment for me to carefully place my poppy in the grass.

The Arcade, off Market Square, was a fascinating warren of offices and small shops. There were several grand looking milliners, dressmakers, tailors and florists but the favourite of many children in Northampton (and their dads) was a small joke shop. It was crammed full with all sorts of practical jokes - spiders and other small creepies to startle people with, fake ink spillages, large nails that looked as if they had gone through the finger, suitably blood stained, soap that was supposed to blacken the skin, all sorts too numerous to list. Some I was allowed to buy and many I would have loved to but was forbidden. I never got to try out the soap on anyone, that was at the top of the forbidden list. We bought quite a few indoor fireworks to use at Christmas parties. Some were quite spectacular but a lot were disappointing and just fizzled away to nothing. I suspect they would all be banned now but I never heard of anyone being hurt by them. The whole Arcade was a joy to visit and it was a very sad day for Northampton when it was demolished. The ordinary folk of the town wanted to keep it but stood no chance against the planners.

Abington Street had some wonderful shops. A tailors shop on the Market Square corner, I think it was called 'The 50 shilling Tailors' had several dummies in the windows. I liked the plump one which Dad had christened Fatty Arbuckle, I found out years after, that there was a film star of that name.

On the other side of the road was Kingham's grocery store where one window was given over to the roasting and grinding of coffee beans - a delicious aroma! Inside the store each counter had chairs set in front so that the customer could sit while the assistant took and made up her order. It all looked very grand and much later in my life after I married in 1950, I received the same treatment from the Kettering Road branch of James Brothers and enjoyed it a lot. Customers could choose the thickness of bacon and how many slices. Dry goods, sugar, tea, dried fruit etc. were weighed and put into blue or brown bags. Is it just nostalgia or did they really taste much better than the pre-packed goods that came later?

Wiggins coal merchants was nearby and their window had on display a row of small bowls/baskets, each containing samples of different sorts of coal. Not a speck of coal dust anywhere!

We got our coal from Wardens in Harlestone Road but quite often we would buy cheaper coke from the gas works. Dad would get a lovely fire going, starting it with coal and then banking it up with the coke so that it burned with a red hot glow. It was perfect for toasting crumpets or bread and I was always happy to take on this task.

Mum always sat as close as she could to the fire and as a result the sides of her legs were etched with a honeycomb of red. They faded a bit in the summer but never went completely and eventually the deepest marks turned to purple. Goodness knows what happened to the veins in her legs.

During very cold weather our fire was kept in all night by banking up the grate with coal 'slack'. It smouldered through the night and just needed a poke or two in the morning to get a good blaze. The warm room was very welcome on frosty mornings.

Once a year a carnival parade took place in the town, to raise money for the General Hospital. It was originally called the Cycle Parade as those taking part either walked with or rode decorated cycles. Prizes were given to the best dressed and most original. I can just remember taking part in my dancing teacher's, Grace Wootton's display. This was on a decorated flat back lorry as, by this time, both lorries and motorised vehicles were taking part, as well as the cycles and walking entries. The procession went all round the town centre and then through lots of side streets further out of the town, finishing near to Abington Park. Throngs of people turned out to watch all along the route. They all threw money onto the floats or put it into collecting tins and it was great fun with the entrants working really hard to part the spectators from their pennies. I was only about three or four when I took part so I found it a bit scary to have money flying at our lorry - coins hurt a bit if they hit you but it was all in a good cause and in those days a lot of money was raised.

The Parade was always held on a Thursday evening as this was early closing day in Northampton and all the shops closed at lunch time.

Chapter Eight

Illness and Hospitals

The first illness that I became aware of was when Papa Ives had pneumonia in the early 1930s. When we visited I wasn't allowed in the bedroom and had to be very quiet downstairs. Everyone was solemn and spoke in low voices, sometimes in whispers. He was seriously ill and the doctor visited many times. His fever was very high and by listening to what my elders were saying I found out that he was reaching 'the crisis' when either the fever would break or he would die. I don't know how long it took or how it was achieved but thankfully the fever eventually broke and he started to recover. Needless to say everyone was relieved, especially poor Nan, and conversation was restored to normal tones. Eventually I was allowed to see him for a short time and he looked very thin and pale in the big feather bed.

Our childish ailments were quite simply treated with old fashioned remedies and Mum never made a lot of fuss. With a bad cold, maybe with a temperature, we were put to bed with a stone hot water bottle at our feet to encourage us to 'sweat it out'. If a sore throat made eating difficult we would be fed bread and milk. This was quite nice, thick slices of bread mashed up in warm milk and then liberally sprinkled with brown sugar.

I don't remember having the usual childish illnesses such as measles, mumps and chickenpox etc as Geoff caught all of them and passed them on to me when I was very young. I have a faint memory of having whooping cough which was horrible. The coughing quite often made me sick. Mum told me that I had the typical cough and much to her embarrassment went on 'whooping ' long after I'd passed the infectious stage.

The only illness Geoff didn't pass on to me was scarlet fever and I think Mum nursed him at home. I don't remember being told that he was sent to the Isolation Hospital.

There were no MMR inoculations in our childhood but early on smallpox vaccinations were compulsory for babies. Geoff had his but Mum refused to let me have it. It might have been that she didn't want me to have the scar on my arm or that Geoff had a bad reaction. She never told me why, but not very much later compulsion was stopped and parents could choose whether or not to have their children vaccinated.

I have mentioned that I was admitted to hospital with meningitis when I was a baby but, of course, I don't remember that.

My next experience of hospital came in 1936, just before my eighth birthday.

I had been sent to stay with Nan and Papa (Ives) but wasn't told why. The day after I arrived Dad came to see me and took me for a walk. He seemed quite ill at ease and eventually, to my great surprise, he told me that I now had a baby brother. I was stunned and said the first thing that came into my head, that I really wanted a baby sister, which was a complete nonsense as I had no idea at all that Mum was expecting a baby.

A day or two later I was taken home to meet baby Brian but unfortunately, although I adored babies, I couldn't get very thrilled as I was beginning to feel unwell with a sore throat.

Back with Nan I started to feel worse with a very sore throat and a splitting headache. Nan dosed me with the usual home remedies, hot lemon juice plus the old-fashioned cure-all, a laxative but to no avail. I just got worse and worse.

One afternoon I was in bed and 'saw' a bearded man dressed in a long white robe standing at the foot of the bed. He told me that I was going to die. I immediately told him that I wasn't but he kept insisting that I would. At this point, in spite of the sore throat, I started to scream which brought Nan rushing upstairs to me. The 'man' disappeared as Nan hugged me and I sobbed out my story. I think she was almost as frightened as me and, coupled with the fact that I could no longer swallow the tiny cascara tablets she was dosing me with, sent for the doctor. I had been ill for over a week!

When the doctor arrived he examined me and left, only to return quite soon to give me an injection. He turned me over to inject into my rear end saying "You are going to be brave aren't you". I had been brought up never to make a fuss so I didn't yell when the very painful injection went in. This seemed to worry him somewhat as he quickly peered over to look at me and I should imagine he was quite relieved to see the tears streaming down my face. Apparently I was extremely ill with diphtheria and he had decided to give me a double dose of the serum in an effort to save me.

My mother told me years later that an enquiry was held when Dr Wilson had to defend his decision. The board ruled that my parents had to pay for the extra dose. Dr Wilson also told Mum that he knew I had diphtheria as soon as he entered the house as the illness had a distinctive smell.

Dr Wilson left and Nan told me that I had to go to hospital but I hardly had time to get used to the idea when two very cheerful ambulance men arrived. I was wrapped in a big red blanket and carried out to the green ambulance, which was known by Northampton folk as the 'fever cart'. This transported me to the Isolation Hospital in Harborough Road. Nan wasn't allowed to come with me and I felt very alone and afraid.

On arrival I was put to bed in a ward that had girls at one end and boys at the other, separated by bathrooms and toilets and what we call today, the nurses station. There were two girls already there and they did their best to make me welcome. One of them brought over a comic but when I tried to lift my head to look at it a nurse rushed over and took it away telling me not to move. That was very bewildering and frightened both me and my would-be friend who gave up any further attempt to befriend me.

The treatment was for complete bed rest, lying absolutely flat and not being allowed to do anything for myself. Washing, feeding, drinking and toileting was all taken over by the nurses. I was dosed with a very pleasant warm, brown coloured medicine which I began to look forward to. For a long time I was indifferent to anything else, this lethargy apparently is a symptom of the disease.

Visiting days were Wednesday and Saturday afternoons and as no one except staff was allowed in the ward, visitors, only two allowed, had to come to the windows where any communication was carried out by shouting through the glass.

On the first day I watched the visitors arrive but no one came to my window. As time went by and it became clear that I would have no visitor I tried desperately to think of other things to try to avoid breaking down in tears. After a while a nurse came to sit with me and told me that my mother wouldn't be visiting me for a while as she was too busy with my baby brother. I wasn't to know that visits were banned because I was too ill to stand any excitement.

The weeks passed and very slowly I began to improve with progress measured by being allowed one pillow, then two until, at last, I was allowed to sit up for a while. The real red letter day was when I was able to get out of bed and, all wrapped up in a blanket, was allowed to sit out in a chair. It seemed ages before my legs felt less jelly-like. As I improved so the doses of my favourite medicine were gradually discontinued but I couldn't understand the amusement of the doctor and nurses when I asked if they had forgotten to give it to me. A very long time afterwards I found out that the medicine was in fact warm brandy with sugar in it.

Each time the doctor did his rounds with Sister in attendance, we would eagerly wait to see if he would move us on to another stage of recovery. We children loved Dr Rowlands and I rather think that the nurses were fond of him too. Progress was very slow but it was impressed on us that we must do as we were told or we would 'drop down dead'. True to a point maybe as I now know that diphtheria affects the heart and sudden death is a possibility but it hardly seems the thing to frighten a child with.

It was as well we didn't know of this danger as, during one night, we were awakened by the sound of fire engines in the grounds of the hospital. We all stood up in our beds to look out of the windows trying to see what was happening but couldn't see anything and we had to quickly get down as we heard the approach of Sister and Doctor Rowlands to check on us. I lay very still and feigned sleep but had a job to keep up the pretence when they came to my bedside and discussed whether I was truly asleep or, as they put it, foxing. We had to keep up the pretence the next morning when we were asked if we had heard anything during the night. I think they knew what we had been up to but luckily none of us had any ill effects from the excitement.

I had my eighth birthday in March and everyone tried to make it a happy day. The nurses gave me a birthday tea with a special cake. Cards had arrived and a few presents but I only had the presents with me for the one day. They were then taken away and put in a cupboard with a lot of other toys and games. I was told that they were there so that all children could use them but in all the twelve weeks I was in the hospital none of us had any toys from the cupboard. Certainly anything that came into the ward had to remain there or be destroyed so as to prevent the spread of infection.

Eventually I was well enough to go outside into the spring sunshine. By this time there were only three of us, two boys and me. We were taken on walks round the grounds but couldn't go anywhere near the other block as that housed scarlet fever patients. If the weather was fine enough, the Sister allowed us to have our tea outside. The grounds of the hospital were beautiful and there were daffodils in bloom in the grassy areas round the trees. To this day I prefer to see daffodils growing in grass rather than regimented rows.

Two consecutive throat swabs, a procedure I hated, had to be clear before we could be discharged. In my case this took a long time which accounted for the twelve week stay but on the thirteenth week the happy day came. My mother had to deliver a complete set of clothes for me, as those I had been wearing during my stay had to remain at the hospital, but before I could change into them I had to have a special bath. This was always called an Izal bath because of the disinfectant put in it and once bathed I wasn't allowed back into the ward area. At last I was able to say my goodbyes and thanks to the nurses when my mother collected me and took me home, still a little weak but thankful to be free.

When I wrote to the hospital to thank them for their care of me I was delighted to receive an answer together with a snapshot of me with the two boys and Sister taken when we had tea outside in the sunshine. It was signed "With Dr Rowland's best wishes".

Birthday tea at the Isolation Hospital in Harborough Road – aged 8

I was disappointed when I found I had to go back to stay with Nan Ives instead of going home. My baby brother had problems with feeding and screamed with pain most of the day and night. My poor mother didn't feel able to cope with both of us as Mum, Dad and Geoff weren't getting much sleep, and it was decided that it wouldn't help my convalescence to be at home.

I wasn't allowed to do much because of possible damage to my heart so I spent a lot of time reading and going on short walks with Nan. She let me go out in the street to mix with the children living nearby but they wouldn't come anywhere near me as they were afraid of catching the 'fever'. I tried telling them that they couldn't catch anything from me because I had had an Izal bath which of course, didn't mean anything to them, but they kept taunting me and running away. I was quite upset and had to go in to tell Nan that no-one would play with me.

Whilst in hospital we always sang Grace before meals. It went

Thank you for the world so sweet
Thank you for the food we eat
Thank you for the birds that sing
Thank you God for everything

I loved it and Nan and Papa encouraged me to continue. I was happy to do so until after a few visits from Geoff, when he would mimic me in a silly voice before dissolving into helpless laughter. I was well used to his teasing but eventually I decided not to sing it any more. In any case I was having a job not to laugh with him!

I was eventually sent to stay with Aunt Norah and Uncle Ben in Newport, Essex and stayed there for about a month having a lovely time in the country. I got a bit homesick from time to time but there was always lots of ways to pass the time.

Mum and Dad came to visit, without Brian, which was a bit of a mistake on their part as seeing them again made me yearn to go home with them. Mum tried to dissuade me, telling me that Brian cried almost non-stop and I wouldn't get any peace, but I insisted that I wouldn't mind and kept pleading to go home with them. Part of me wanted to stay with Aunt Norah as I told her, not wanting to hurt her feelings, but I really wanted to see my little brother again because I'd only spent a few minutes with him just after he was born.

I got my way and was taken home where I soon found that I should have listened to Mum's warnings. Poor Brian didn't just cry, he screamed and screamed, nothing would pacify him and he only stopped when he exhausted himself and fell asleep for a short time. There was nothing wrong with his lungs, even the neighbours could hear him. I slept in a back bedroom and Brian was with my parents in the front of the house, the other end of the landing. I used to stick my head under the pillow and when that didn't deaden the sound of his screams I used to wish there were doors all along the passage so that I could shut each one. Geoff slept in the room next to Mum's so he must have suffered worse than me.

The problem was with his stomach and he couldn't take his food so he was getting thinner and thinner. His head looked far too big for his skinny little body with his stick like arms and legs.

Eventually he was taken into hospital and Mum was told that he had a 'twisted gut'. He was kept in for several weeks while the problem was sorted. My parents must have been very worried but probably also quite relieved to be free from the continual screaming. Mum told me, many years later, that once, when she felt she could take no more, she put him on the settee surrounded with cushions and left the house. She felt that if she had stayed she might have harmed him in some way. She must have been so desperate and frustrated at being unable to pacify him.

The day Brian was allowed to come home Mum and Dad took his pram to the hospital to collect him. They put me in it and Dad pushed me all the way there. I loved it and I was excited about Brian coming home. Mum and Dad were happy too and I suppose I was pushed in the pram because they were keen to get him back and I couldn't walk fast enough. Brian was still a puny little fellow and his head still looked far too big for his body, but to our great joy he wasn't crying and was full of smiles. We had never seen him smiling before and the novelty made us all so happy. His problems had all been sorted out and after trying him on several different milk foods it

My brother Brian aged about 1 year old

66

had been found that he tolerated bottled Co-op milk best. He soon picked up strength and developed into a bonny baby. Mum always said that he was a great advert for the Co-op.

I was very proud of him and loved to take him out in his pram. I still hadn't been allowed to go back to school after the diphtheria so one day I persuaded Mum to let me take Brian to my school to show him to my teachers. They must have been a little surprised to see me arrive with him but they must have been extremely shocked when I got him out of his pram and dropped him! So was I but they helped me scoop him up and strap him back in his seat. I rushed home with him and I didn't dare tell Mum what had happened - I never did. Luckily Brian didn't seem too bothered and didn't cry much and by the time I got home he was all smiles and giggles.

My mother had a bad facial rash and was eventually referred to a London hospital as an inpatient to try to find the cause and, more importantly, the cure.

I think I was only about seven years old so once again Nan Ives took over my care, Dad and Geoff looked after themselves. It was said that they ate a lot of baked beans on toast so I must have had the best deal.

Dad told me one day that I could go with him to see Mum in hospital and he got very cross when I didn't want to go. I made the stupid excuse that I would miss the serial at a childrens' cinema matinee instead of admitting to the real reason, that I was afraid of crying on leaving Mum all that way away.

Of course I had to go and I managed not to upset myself and Mum by crying.

I only went that once as Mum was discharged soon afterwards. I believe it was decided her skin rash was rosacia but she was embarrassed by it for a long time afterwards. This was before antibiotics and she used to use calamine lotion a lot. It eventually cleared up without ever finding the cause.

I used to walk up Wellingborough Road on my way to see Nan and Papa which took me past the Workhouse, later called St Edmunds

Hospital. In fine weather there were usually physically disabled patients sitting outside the lodge at the outside gate. One of these, named Philip was well known in town. He always had a smile and a cheery word for passers by even though he was flat on his back in a spinal carriage and was a permanent patient at the hospital. The others were all in wheel chairs but they made a very cheerful group.

Each day in the late afternoon a queue of homeless men could be seen waiting for the Casual Ward of the Workhouse to open at 6 pm to make sure of a meal and bed for the night. It was quite sad to see so many of them.

Not an illness exactly but one awful day I had an appointment with the school dentist to have a tooth extracted. There was nothing wrong with it but I was told I had too many permanent teeth coming through.

It was an awful experience as I was given gas with no explanation of what was to happen. A horrible rubber mask was pushed over my nose and mouth and I was told to breathe deeply. The dentist was not very pleased with me as my first reaction was to struggle and hold my breath. I suppose I was only unconscious for a few minutes and I came to with my mouth full of blood. My mother took me over to a basin to rinse most of the blood away and I had to mop up the rest with a huge handkerchief.

On my way to the basin I could see other children going through the same ordeal. As fast as a child left the dentist's chair another one was put in.

I don't recall any child crying but if they were anything like me they were too much in shock from the procedure.

Chapter Nine

Back to School

At last life got back to normal after suffering from diphtheria. I was taken for many check-up visits to Dr Wilson but at last he allowed me to 'go out to play' and, best of all, I could go swimming again. He must have advised Mum to give me a tonic to build up my strength as she started to dose me with cod liver oil and malt, a horrible concoction, so thick, oily and sticky that it clung round my mouth for ages. After the first doses I tried all sorts of tricks to avoid taking any more, all to no avail. I used to insist that I really was better and didn't need to take it but, three times a day, out came the dreaded jar and Mum would plunge in a big spoon in the gooey mixture and attempt to push it into my mouth. I tried to keep my lips tightly shut but as she tried to force the spoon into my mouth some of the mixture came off and dribbled down my chin and on to my clothes. She was furious. One day the same pantomime was about to start and I changed tactics. I forced myself to cry. This time Dad was home and he took me on his lap, giving me the impression that I had won. I waited for him to comfort me but he didn't say a word and to my horror he turned me over his knee and spanked me, hard. It was the first time I had been treated like that, but I have to admit now that I really deserved it. As he passed me back to Mum my mouth must have been open with shock as I swallowed the dose without making any more fuss. In fact, I never played up any more after that.

I had missed the last terms of Infant school but, nevertheless, in September I moved up to the girls department of St James Junior School. I was put into Miss Cakebread's class and she was so different to the nice teachers I had known at Spencer Infants. One of the first lessons I had with her was arithmetic and she set us some sums in 'long division'. I had missed all the teaching of this because of my long absence before the holiday and I just had no idea of how to start. I tried in vain to explain why I couldn't do the sums but she wouldn't listen and had me out to the front of the class, saying that I was either lazy or a dunce. Luckily this was the last lesson before the dinner break and the bell saved me from further humiliation. I went home but I was too miserable to eat my lunch and when my mother told me it was time to go back to school I told her that I wasn't going any more. Even though I felt really upset and a bit frightened, I daren't cry but just held my ground and insisted that I wasn't ever going back. Mum couldn't understand it as I had always loved school but eventually she persuaded me to tell her the problem, whereupon she let me stay home but put on her coat and off she went to the school. She must have been furious! When she came back she assured me that she had sorted it out with both the Head and Miss Cakebread and I was to go to school as usual the next day. I was still nervous and dreaded the next morning. Miss Cakebread set sums as usual and then came to my desk to explain how to do them. She held a big ruler and with a fixed smile on her face said that I should have told her why I couldn't do long division sums.(I had). Then, still smiling, she rapped me with the ruler hard, across the back of my hand, trying to make it seem like a big joke. Eventually I caught up with the work I'd missed but I never really enjoyed going to St James School again.

The class rooms were very old fashioned and in the winter they were heated by a solid fuel stove in the corner behind a cast iron rail. Our milk bottles were brought in with the frozen milk pushing up through the cardboard tops, so they were put in front of the stove to thaw out before morning break. The milk was usually warm by then.

A brass plate was on the wall of the class room in memory of twins, Gladys and Lily Gammons who were killed, with their mother, in their home in Parkwood Street as a result of a zepplin air raid in 1917. I suppose the twins were pupils of the school. It was my first experience of what war could do to ordinary people and I found it so very sad.

Although my love of school was spoiled and I came to dread the arithmetic lessons, I still very much enjoyed English lessons and I became an avid reader. It was a great joy when I was old enough to join the Library on St James Square which was a branch of the town library in Abington Street. It occupied a large room above a butchers shop and the Bank, and was reached by a steep flight of stone steps at the side of the butchers' shop. The childrens' section was tucked away to the left of the librarian's desk putting her in the ideal position to hush any child who dared to speak too loudly. I loved the whole atmosphere of it, the smell of the books and the air of silence, almost like a church. My favourite fiction books at that time were the 'William' series by Richmal Crompton and I must have read them all. Other books I loved included the Katy series by Susan Coolidge, another series, Little Women by Louisa Allcot and the Water Babies by Kingsley.

I think it was in 1938 that we moved house to Abington at the other end of town. I was not very happy to leave my friends but I didn't mind at all leaving St James junior school and Miss Cakebread.

Chapter Ten

Life in Abington

Our first house in Abington was semi-detached and the very last one in Broadway East. I thought it was wonderful and loved the fact that we had a garden front, side and back, but best of all, we had a proper bathroom and an indoor toilet.

I now attended the Headlands Junior School which was a complete contrast to St James. The entrance was approached by a large playing field and the building was modern and airy. After the Victorian built school I had been used to, my new school was such a pleasure, and I loved it.

I soon made a lot of new friends and settled in happily. The teachers were very nice too and for the first time I was taught by a man. Two of them, Mr Skelton and Mr Chambers, always arrived at school together. Mr Skelton was fairly plump and jolly, Mr Chambers was a lot smaller and quieter but both always greeted us pleasantly as they passed.

My little brother Brian, now a toddler, enjoyed having a bigger garden to play in but one memorable day he caused a panic when he decided to explore farther afield. He was nowhere to be found in the garden and as the gate was open Mum was horrified to realise that he had gone out into the street. We all went up and down calling out his name but there was no sign of him. There was a building site on the other side of the road and I thought I heard a cry from that direction. It was weekend so no builders were on site and sure enough when I went to look I found a very tearful Brian under the floor joists of one of the partly built houses. He had climbed or fallen down and as he was so little, he couldn't get out. He looked so pathetic with tear tracks down his very dusty face but he soon got over it after I lifted him out and took him back to Mum. We were all so relieved that he was safe as he had crossed the road, to get to the buildings. After that the gate had an extra childproof fastening but I don't remember Brian ever trying to go out again.

There were more mishaps during our time at Broadway East.

Geoff, by this time was attending the Boys' Grammar School in Billing Road and cycled there. He was playing in a cricket match one afternoon and set off on his cycle resplendent in his cricket 'whites', spotless flannels, white shirt and his school blazer. It was quite a shock to see him limping back, wheeling his damaged bike and with his clothes heavily bloodstained. He had been cycling along at a fair speed past a building site and had hit a brick in the road. He was thrown head first over the handlebars into the road, cutting his head quite badly and hurting his knees too. His flannels were in holes and ruined. I was left to look after Brian while Geoff was taken off to the Hospital to have his head stitched. He had to go back to the hospital after a few days to be checked and this time I went with them, together with Brian in his push chair. We had got well on the way when Mum suddenly realized she had left the appointment card at home. I checked which way they would be walking and said I would run back for it and catch them up. Unfortunately Mum went a different route to the one we'd agreed on and I didn't catch them up until we were just outside the Hospital. I was out of breath as I'd run all the way and Mum had been worried thinking I was lost.

I was the next casualty. I was missing my friends in St James End so one Saturday afternoon Mum let me go by bus to visit them. A group of us had a happy reunion and after a while made our way to the fields where we used to play. The footpath ran along the top of a steep incline leading to a barbed wire fence round the field. We decided to go down into the field and one of the girls and myself overbalanced and tumbled down the slope. I finished up straddled over the fence with Nancy on top of me. Her weight drove me into the barbed wire which embedded deeply into my leg. It was a sickening sensation as I struggled free and felt the wire tearing at my flesh. I had numerous cuts and scratches but the worst injuries were to my left leg which bled profusely. Nancy was luckier and only got a few scratches. My friends helped me off the wire and took me to the nearby house of one of the group. I guess her parents must have been shocked at the sight of me, bleeding all over their kitchen. They sent along for one of their neighbours who was a policeman and he stopped the bleeding and bandaged my leg. They also sent word to our good neighbour in Lincoln Road, Mrs. Allen, who came at once. With her husband they put me into a child's pushchair and took me to the hospital. Once in the accident department I was put on a table and examined by a doctor. He really upset me as he was holding up some of my clothes with remarks like 'I think this was once a dress'. I hadn't realized that my clothes were so badly torn and it was then that I started to cry as I thought my mother would be really cross. I cried a lot more when the doctor started to stitch the worst injury in the calf of my leg. No pain relief at all, the nurses held me down while he dug the needle in deeply. It was a gaping hole so there was no chance of closing it fully so I have been left with a large scar on the calf and lesser ones the length of my leg. It would have been a lot worse if I hadn't been able to keep my face clear of the barbed wire.

When I was all stitched and bandaged Mr. and Mrs. Allen put me back in the pushchair and walked all the way home to Abington, which was quite a long way. They were such good friends.

I couldn't get about much as my leg was bandaged from top to bottom so I was off school. It was very boring. When the date of my follow-up appointment at the hospital came round I persuaded Mum to let me go by myself. I convinced her that it would be better than her having to take Brian with us and that as the bus terminus was outside our gate, and I knew the way, I could manage. As I was first on the bus I was able to sit on one of the long seats just inside and drape my leg along it. The conductor teased me about it and we had a laugh but he was very helpful when I got off, lifting me off the platform and on to the pavement. I then hobbled along to the accident department and waited for my turn. A lady was also waiting and wanted to know what had happened to me. She then gave me half a crown (12½p) for being, as she put it, very brave. It was a lot of money then and I tried to refuse it. I was almost too amazed to thank her when she insisted I took it.

My turn came to see the doctor who undid all the bandages and after checking everything just bandaged my lower leg, which was a relief. He was a tease too and we had a good laugh. On the next appointment he took out the stitches. That hurt but not as much as when they went in!

Chapter Eleven

Abington and Back to St James

In 1938 the threat of war loomed, which worried everyone. I didn't fully understand it all and found it quite exciting to see searchlights sweeping across the sky as the Army crews practiced. Eventually 'The Crisis' passed but when I asked my parents if there was to be a war, they just said 'Not this time'. There was no television then so I suppose they had heard on the radio of Mr Chamberlain returning from Munich and saying that there would be no war in our time.

We moved soon after this to another nice house in Bushland Road, not very far away so I didn't have to change schools this time. We were only a short distance from the countryside and my friend, Barbara, and I went for walks or bike rides in Booth Lane. We were able to pick lots of blackberries in the fields alongside and it was all beautiful. The lane led to an area called Buttocks Booth, a name which we found hilarious. The whole area is built up now and they don't use that name anymore.

One day on one of our bike rides Barbara took a tumble and cut herself quite badly. I took her to our house but Mum wasn't in so I bathed her cut and then went home with her. I didn't think to wipe up all the blood from the basin so my poor mother arrived home to find me missing and the blood stains. I really got told off when I got back.

The garden of our house wasn't much good for growing as it was mainly very heavy clay, so much so that I was able to take a handful and mould it into shapes. Dad had tried to dig it without success and the ground was extremely uneven.

One afternoon, after I got home from school, Mum was in the garden starting to hang out washing on the line and because it was set so high she fetched a stool to stand on. The inevitable happened, the stool tipped, throwing her to the ground and she broke her arm. I was indoors and was shocked to see her come in all white and shaken, nursing a badly deformed arm with the broken bone sticking out. I wanted to go back to school to ask Mr Skelton for help as I knew he was a St John's Ambulance member. She said I was not to but as she was nearly fainting I took no notice and went. Luckily he was still in the school and he came to see what he could do. I can't exactly remember how, but he got her to the hospital. I was left with Brian to wait for Dad to come home and to tell him what had happened. He rushed to the hospital at once and eventually brought Mum home with her arm in plaster. Her wrist was very badly fractured and she never got the full use of it after that.

We hadn't been at Bushland Road very long when two men (I found out a lot later that they were detectives) came to the door and Dad had to go away with them. This left Mum trying not to cry and me not knowing what to say or do to comfort her. I was glad that Brian was too young to understand and I think Geoff wasn't home when this happened. Dad came back a lot later in the day, elated and telling Mum how good the police had been. This didn't cheer her up at all and they went off into another room to discuss it all. To this day I don't know what it was about except that it was some sort of money trouble. Unfortunately this was the start of realizing that my Dad wasn't as perfect as I'd always thought

I don't know if it was because of this trouble Dad had got into but soon after that we had yet another move. This time it was back to St James, a council house in Baring Road. Mum was very upset about it, I suppose she thought it was a comedown but in a way I was quite glad as my best friend lived in a council house and had always sneered at me because I didn't.

It was a lovely sunny day when we moved in and I thought the house was very nice. It was semi-detached with a garden in the front and a very long one at the back. A path ran at the end of all the gardens and beyond that was a fresh water stream with water cress growing in it. On the other side of that were allotments which made the area seem quite rural.

This move didn't entail a change of school for me as I had reached the age of taking the 'Scholarship Exam', the forerunner of the 11 plus. Our house in Bushland Road was just outside the borough boundary so I had already taken an exam for county children for entry to the Northampton High School. Now we had moved back into the borough I had to take another exam! It was decided that I should stay at The Headlands School until the exams were over so, during the week, I stayed with my grandparents in Adnitt Road. It was still quite a distance to get to school so I was allowed to cycle – four times a day as there were no school dinners in those days. Nan was very good and always had my dinner on the table so that I could get back to school in good time.

The exams were over and I had found the county papers were much easier than the borough. However I passed both and then had to go to the Northampton School or Girls with the three other girls from my school, to take an 'Oral'. We were called into the Library in turn and were given tests at four different tables. The one I most readily recall was that I was shown a series of pictures and told to continue the story in my own words. I found that enjoyable as I loved stories but, on the whole, the solemn atmosphere in the room was a bit overpowering and it was hard to relax.

Successful pupils of the Scholarship Exam at Headlands Junior School

When the results came through I had passed both exams and it now had to be decided which High School I would be attending. The education board finally decided that, as we now lived in the borough, I should go to the Northampton School for Girls. The notification of their decision arrived together with the permit to buy the school uniform and details of the shops where it was to be bought. Some of the items were available at Carne's, and the rest at Saundersons, both school outfitters. It was all very exciting but it must have been a huge expense to my parents as they also had to buy uniform for Geoff at the Grammar School. The one thing I had always wanted was the blazer, very smart in navy with black and white braiding. I was really happy to at last own one.

The rest of the uniform consisted of a navy blue gym slip to be worn over a white square necked blouse. For Speech Days and other functions we wore a skirt with a cream blouse of silky material and a striped tie. The stripes were coloured red, blue, green or yellow. We couldn't buy the ties until we were at the school and knew which house colour we needed. The winter coats were navy and worn with a navy velour hat trimmed with a band of the school colours and the school badge in front. We had a panama hat in the summer with the same trim. Our shoes had to be navy of course but we also had to have softer and lighter indoor shoes.

Northampton School for Girls

Speech day at NSG. I am at the back, 5th from the right

For tennis we had grey shorts and white plimsols, the forerunner of trainers, but nothing like them. Our gym shoes were black plimsols. For hockey we had special ankle boots which gave some protection from the hard hockey ball.

All these things as well as the satchels and shoe bags had to be marked so I had a long session of sewing in Cash's name tapes.

It was, as I said, exciting but I was disappointed that my best friend Barbara had to go to The Convent School. I would have liked to have gone with her. Once we left the Headlands we went our different ways and never met up again.

The blazer I had been so happy to wear led to a spot of unpleasantness. I was walking with Brian when a much bigger girl came up to me and started to pull at the blazer, accusing me of being 'stuck up'. I decided to ignore her remarks and tried to walk on but she then started to punch me. I hit her back but before it became a real fight Brian started to cry. I was really cross with her for frightening him and told her what a bully she was and to leave us both alone. To my amazement, she did and I was able to comfort Brian but it was some time before I stopped shaking.

Geoff wasn't so pleased with his school uniform as he had to wear a straw hat, called a boater, and stiff collars in the style of Eton public school. He also had to wear short trousers and wouldn't be allowed to wear long ones until reaching the age of thirteen. He was a stocky build and the short trousers were very tight round his thighs but the school stuck rigidly to this rule for many years.

The boater he could tolerate even though it was a game for younger boys to jump up and tip it off his head. His friend hated his and when he was bought a new one he rubbed dirt into it and punched it. He went a bit too far and finished up with a hole in it and was in dire trouble from his parents.

The collars were a real menace for Geoff as the constant rubbing from them on his neck resulted in awful boils. They had to be poulticed until they burst and Mum then had to bathe them to get rid of the pus. She was doing this one day and had asked me to hold a torch so that she could see better. The look of his neck and the awful smell of the pus horrified me and Mum noticed that the torch light had developed a definite wobble. She took one look at my green face and quickly relieved me of my duty before she had two patients.

After I got my uniform Mum took me to the photographers for a picture of me all dressed up. I had set my heart on having a pair of leather gauntlet gloves and I had them on for the photo. They must have been a birthday present or maybe a present for obtaining the scholarship.

In my smart school uniform

I had got very fond of visiting Abington Park when we lived in Abington, and one winter's day I went with my friend Daphne to the big lake there, one of three. It was frozen over and lots of people were skating on the ice. We went on it just sliding as neither of us had the luxury of ice skates. The ice was thinner round the edges of the lake and there was just one place where it was thick enough to get on and off the ice. We had great fun but when it was time to leave there was a queue to get off so as we got a bit impatient we decided that another spot looked safe. I went first and realized we had made a bad mistake when the ice cracked and I went right through it soaking the bottom of my coat and skirt. The worst thing was that as I tried to save myself by reaching out to the bank, my lovely gauntlet gloves filled with the ice cold water. I was lucky that the water wasn't deeper. We went to Daphne's house where I tried to dry myself before I caught the bus home but my gloves were ruined. They dried but were left all stiff, this was fine for the gauntlet but not for the rest of the gloves. Mum was cross about it and I didn't get a replacement so I had to go back to woollen gloves.

Rug making became a family pastime and although it was a very good winter activity it went on for a long time after. I'm not sure who started doing the rugs first but soon Mum, Nan Ives and some of the aunts were devoting their evenings to producing various rugs.

The method they used was latch hook rug making and one could buy kits consisting of canvas mesh, stenciled or painted with a design or picture, wool and of course the special latch hook tool.

The wool was either bought in ready cut bundles or as a ball with a tool to cut your own. This was a wooden bar with a groove on the side and the wool was wound all round it and then cut through the groove. This method gave you the correct lengths for the rug making and was cheaper than the ready cut bundles.

I joined in the sessions by first being allowed to wind and cut the wool and eventually being taught how to join wool to canvas with the latch hook. This was done by first looping each strand of wool in half and then pushing the hook through the canvas in the appropriate hole, hooking the wool onto the end and drawing it through to make two tufts of the pattern. It was very satisfying to see the pattern develop. Once the pattern was finished the rug had to be bound and lined. I left that part to Mum.

We made quite a few rugs and I was sorry when we didn't need any more.

Nan Ives already had rag rugs but I never found out how she made them as she replaced most of them with the latch hook rugs.

Chapter Twelve

Pets & Animal 'Friends'

We had two pets at Lincoln Road, a terrier called Gyp and a cat called Fluff. Both were very good and allowed me to dress them in my doll's clothes and take them for a walk round the garden in my doll's pram. Neither ever scratched and Gyp never growled, in fact I'm sure he liked the fuss and he looked so cute in a bonnet.

Nan Ives had a long haired black cat called Smut which let me brush him but hid under the kitchen table when he was tired of the attention. Nan used to feed him with something called 'lights'. It must have been the insides of an animal but she had to boil it first and the smell as she did this was revolting.

Smut lived to a good old age but I'm not sure what happened to our pets. I was told that Gyp had to be 'put to sleep', a phrase I didn't understand and I was sad that he'd gone but Fluff went with no explanation.

I missed having a pet so I was very happy, when we moved to Abington and I had a new pet, a tortoise I called Joey. I loved him and enjoyed feeding him lettuce leaves and other tortoise food. I made him a bed of straw in a box but he liked to wander in the garden and many times I had to fetch him back from the front of the house. He hibernated and woke up again safely but then one day I couldn't find him anywhere. I never saw him again and we thought he must have wandered back to the front garden and been stolen.

Our bread was delivered by a Co-op baker with a horse drawn van which he left outside our house while he was delivering to several neighbouring houses. I took to feeding his horse every afternoon and the horse began to look forward to his treats. The baker didn't know about this until one day I was a bit late getting to the gate. To my dismay the horse came on to the pavement and headed for our gate. The baker spotted what was happening and rushed back shouting at the horse and pulled the reluctant animal back on the road. I felt so guilty and never fed it again.

I was the cause of another mishap with an animal. A friend of my parents' asked if they would look after their puppy for a few days. I was thrilled to have another 'pet' to spoil and enjoyed playing with him. He was not allowed into the garden in case he got out onto the street but one day I came into the kitchen just in time to see the puppy making his escape through the back door. I rushed over to shut him in but unfortunately I slammed the door onto his tail and cut part of it clean off. I was horrified and the poor dog was squealing in shock. His tail was bandaged and he was fussed by all of us and seemed to recover quite quickly. Mum and Dad had the task of telling the puppy's owners what had happened when they came to collect him. I kept out of the way but I wasn't told off much as Mum and Dad could see how it had happened and I hadn't left the door open in the first place.

I made new friends at Baring Road and one of them told me that she had some baby guinea pigs that needed a home. I went to see them and fell in love with them so I then had the task of persuading Mum to let me have two of them. I'd already chosen the names, Pip and Squeak which were the names of characters from a newspaper's daily cartoon. There was a third character, Wilfred and I would have loved to have had the complete set but although Mum had given in to my pleading to have two, there was no way she would let me have three. They were albinos, white with pink eyes and I thought they were sweet but Mum said they looked like rats and shuddered at the sight of them. They soon settled into the hutch Dad made for them and tucked into the food I gave them.

One day one of them wouldn't eat and was squeaking all the time. He seemed to be in a lot of pain. I didn't know what to do but Nan Britten arrived on one of her visits and she took over. She gave the guinea pig a dose of whisky and decided to take him to the PDSA surgery in town. Pip (or was it Squeak) was popped into a box and off we went where he was examined thoroughly by a very nice vet, who then broke it to me gently that I'd been overfeeding the poor thing. I felt so guilty! I cut down on their food and both the guinea pigs were much better. The vet didn't make a charge so Nan put a donation in the PDSA collecting box.

Later on Dad got two pet baby rabbits, a white one for me and a black one for Brian. We loved them but didn't know we had two bucks and unfortunately, when they got older and bigger they started to fight each other. During one vicious battle I tried to separate them and got badly bitten. I daren't touch them again after that so they had to go. Dad wanted to kill them and cook them but Brian and I were so upset at this idea that he had to give them away.

Another pet I had was a budgie. My Uncle Frank bred budgies and said that I could pick one for myself. He told me the sex of his latest birds and, because he told me that that it's easier to teach male birds to talk, I chose a pretty blue male and called him Joey. Uncle Frank also gave me a cage, not a fancy one but more like a box with wire mesh at the front. It was very kind of him to take the trouble to educate me about budgies, especially as he never spoke to me much. On reflection, none of the husbands of my great aunts spoke much. I don't know why but this made me a bit shy with them.

Joey was lovely and became quite tame and eventually learnt to talk. He used to bob up and down in front of his mirror and chatter to his reflection. Unfortunately he also learnt to copy the squawks of the crows which Mum hated.

I used to let him out of his cage provided the windows and doors were shut and, one day he gave me a fright... he flew straight into the fire! Luckily the fire was only glowing with no flames and Dad quickly scooped him out. His wing feathers were singed so he couldn't fly for a while but soon recovered and never went near the fire again.

He would often perch on my shoulder or head and nibble my ear. One day he was attracted to my pen as I was doing my homework. He pattered all across the wet ink on my exercise book. I had to apologise to the Mistress for the mess he made. I bet she had never heard that sort of excuse before or since!

After I'd had him for a number of years I decided to save up and get him a fancy cage. I was very pleased when I got it but it was a bad move. His cosy box cage was in the bay window and I put the new cage in the same place, not realizing that it was draughty. It was only a few mornings after that I came in to find poor Joey on his back with claws in the air, stone dead on the floor of his fancy cage. I was heartbroken and felt very guilty that I had unintentionally caused his death. He was buried in the garden with due ceremony and although Uncle Frank offered me another bird I never replaced Joey.

Chapter Thirteen

London, Holiday & Summer Outings

We made visits to London, usually by train but sometimes by car. Again I don't know how we came to travel by road as we didn't own such a luxury so I can only suppose that Dad borrowed one from someone. I enjoyed both ways of getting to the capital and each journey had land marks I always looked for. The route Dad chose took us through Newport Pagnell and then on to Woburn where we would look for the herd of deer kept in the grounds of Woburn Abbey. The next thing to look out for was at Dunstable and we would all scour the skies to spot the gliders flying from the Downs. Farther on the route was the imposing town of St Albans which I always rated as 'nearly there'. Of course once we reached Swiss Cottage, where Dad left the car to travel on by the Underground, we really were in London and various treats were in store for us. Madame Tussauds was a favourite with us and Dad would try and catch me out by sending me to ask a question of an official who, of course, always turned out to be a wax dummy. Sometimes I would stand in front of a figure for ages, not sure if it was a waxwork or a real attendant, and it would always make me jump when it was a man and he suddenly moved. I suppose the officials still play that joke on tourists! I was fascinated by the figure of the Sleeping Beauty who was actually 'breathing' but Geoff and I both loved to go to the Chamber of Horrors where Dad would tell us all the gory details of the murderers and the torture chambers in the tableaux. Mum preferred to give this part a miss and waited upstairs for us.

I believe we had a picnic lunch on the way to London but we always had tea in a Lyons Corner House and were served by the very smart waitresses called 'Nippies'. I remember that the cakes were always delicious and it was extremely hard to make a choice.

Another treat was to go to Selfridge's department store and one memorable day, in the early 1930s, we went to see a demonstration of television in the music department. One part of the area was set up as a studio where we could watch a 'live' performance of a lady singing and then, at the other end of the department we were able to see the performance transmitted on to a television set. It was pure magic for me.

On one visit my parents bought me a doll that could 'walk'- more magic! The doll came up to my waist and I was shown how to hold it under the arms and to slightly lift first one side and then the other. The legs were on some sort of weights and consequently stepped forward, thus 'walking'. I had never seen such a doll and was so happy with it. Alas, a few days after I got home I was allowed to take the doll into the street to show to one of my friends. She begged me to let her make the doll walk and I gave in but then came the calamity. She held it in the wrong position, the doll suddenly folded forward from the top of the legs and the head smashed onto the pavement. Of course it shattered into many pieces - my friend was horrified and I was heartbroken.

I always enjoyed visits to London Zoo and loved the riding on the elephant. Climbing the high steps to get up to the same height as the animal was a bit daunting, even with help from the keeper. From the top we were helped onto the special seat strapped over the elephant's back - I think it held eight, four on each side. A thick band was placed across all the children (not very secure) and we were then taken on a very rocky ride round part of the Zoo. I had a ride on a camel once but I liked 'Jumbo' the best.

The real highlight was the Chimps Tea party. They all sat at a table and enjoyed their food and mugs of tea. There was a bit of food throwing and leaving the table but I suppose that was all part of the act and it was very funny to see them misbehaving with their keepers.

Another enjoyable visit was the Tower which fascinated me. We joined the queue to gaze at the Crown Jewels and marvel at their dazzling precious stones. Dad told me about the Traitors Gate and showed me where executions were carried out outside the Tower. The ravens also fascinated me, especially when I was told that if they ever flew away it meant that England was doomed. I fed them some of my picnic sandwiches and felt that I was encouraging them to stay.

One day I was taken to Downing Street and told that Number 10 was the house where the Prime Minister lived. We waited on the pavement opposite the house and watched the coming and going. I don't remember seeing any well known person arriving or leaving but I was very impressed by the important looking London policeman outside the door and the air of anticipation of the rest of the people waiting with us.

We would stay in London until after dark so that we could see the lights go on. I loved to see all the advertising signs with their animated displays.

I usually slept on the return journey but on one occasion I was too frightened to close my eyes. A typical London fog came down and it was a real 'pea-souper'. We crawled along and at each junction a policeman carrying a flare was trying to get vehicles safely through and shouting "Keep going, keep going" if anyone slowed down too much. Both the front windows were down with Dad leaning out on his side and Geoff out of the other to try and keep us on course. It was all very scary and I can remember hiding my head in Mum's lap and saying "I wish we were home". She answered with feeling, "So do I". Once we were clear of the city visibility was much improved and we were able to pick up speed to get home.

The train journey was, of course, without the hazards of the road and if the weather was fine we would have the window down. This was operated by a wide leather strap with holes in it which could be notched on to a metal projection on the bottom of the window frame. It was easy enough to open the window as the strap was freed which allowed the window to fall. However, to shut it was more difficult, as the strap had to be pulled up and notched on to the last hole. If you missed it or let go too quickly the heavy window went down again with a loud crash. On approaching a tunnel the train driver would sound the whistle and passengers would rush to close the windows. Failure to do this resulted in a soot speckled face and clothes.

The journey was very interesting and I don't know which sort of train I liked best. It was exciting to be on an express and to rush through the stations but on the slower trains I liked the stops at each of the stations and to see the bustle of some passengers getting off and others getting on. Dad would point out the landmarks on the way, the canals and rivers and the different factories. My favourite was the Ovaltine factory and it was always a game to see who could spot it first.

On arrival at Euston we did much the same things as we did when we went by car except we used the Underground more. Of course leaving London was governed by the train times and, if Mum and Dad had done all they wanted to, and there was still a lot of time until the next train, we went to one of the 'News Theatres'. These were cinemas which showed news reels interspersed with cartoons and sometimes, travel films. It was non-stop screening so folk could come and go as they pleased. The cartoons were mostly by Disney, some were called 'Silly Symphonies'. I don't know if they were Disney but some of these were meant to warn children of dangerous games. The one that stuck in my mind was one of a little child who found a box of matches. He found it great fun to light matches one by one but soon dropped one into the open matchbox and ignited the lot, eventually setting the house on fire. This, of course, was a strong warning not to play with fire but it was wasted on me as I was always fascinated by fire.

We had many other outings during the summer months. A visit to the seaside was always fun. Skegness and Hunstanton were the usual favourites as they were the nearest. We went by car and Mum always packed a tasty picnic. My brother Geoff hated picnicking and would stay in the car to eat, even going so far as draping the windows with towels so that no one could see him eating. On one occasion when we ate a meal of fish and chips at a table outside the shop Geoff reached for what he thought was the salt sprinkler. He liberally shook it over his meal only to find, too late, that he had covered his meal with caster sugar. He was the only one who didn't laugh! We all gave him some of our meals so that he didn't go hungry.

One year we had a fortnight's holiday at Great Yarmouth and joined forces with the Steel family so we were quite a large group. They were Ella, my aunt Doll's sister, her husband Arch and their three children, Ray, Madge and Ronnie. We had a caravan for the women and girls. The men and boys had a lean-to tent pitched at the side of the caravan.

Madge and I were about the same age so we spent a lot of time together and on one occasion we were so absorbed digging in the sand that we didn't notice the tide coming in and the sea swirling all round us. Luckily the family saw what was happening and shouted at us to come in before the water got too deep for us to wade through.

During the first week of the holiday a nasty smell was noticed in the tent and there was a search to find the cause after smelly socks/feet had been ruled out. Eventually they discovered a neat row of chewing gum stuck on the side of the caravan which formed one wall of the tent. Geoff had been chewing his gum through the day and each night had stuck it on the caravan before settling down to sleep. The weather was very hot so the gum was deteriorating and getting smellier by the day.

There was a honeymoon couple in a tent on the next site who unwittingly caused a lot of amusement for the adults of our party. They didn't realise that the lamp in their tent threw their shadows to anyone outside and the fellows in our group really enjoyed the nightly show. Madge and I didn't know what the joke was!

We were more amused by another incident involving the honeymooners. The lady wore a very nice hand knitted bathing costume but found out during her first swim that the sea water caused to costume to stretch such a lot that the neck line came down almost to her knees. She daren't come out of the sea and her husband had to go out to her with a towel to save her modesty. We all thought it a great joke!

This holiday was when I was quite young but, although I can only remember isolated snatches, my main memory is of having a wonderful time.

Arch and Ella and children used to join us for swimming at 'Middie Meadow' and for many years I thought we were related to them. We kept in contact with them right into the 1940's.

In the spring a visit to see the tulip fields in bloom was always spectacular. Fields and fields of the different coloured tulips, visible for miles because the fields are in the flat Fenlands, remain a vivid memory of mine.

On one visit we were, as usual, admiring the tulips when Dad stopped the car and got out, I think to take a photo. He had a habit of undoing his trousers at the waist while he was driving and this time forgot to do them up. He got as far as the front of the car before his trousers dropped down round his ankles. Nan Ives who was with us was quite shocked which amused us even more.

Nearer home, probably during our rides in the country, we went near to the huge hangars at Cardington air field and if we were lucky the doors would be open so that we could see the two Airships. They were huge but I didn't fancy flying in one after Dad told me the story of how a German airship called the Hindenburg caught fire during a thunderstorm and crashed in America. A second one, the British R101, crashed in France near Beauvais. In both incidents a lot of people were killed and it seemed a horrible way to die.

Another zoo we visited was Whipsnade where the animals were given more room than at London Zoo. Some of them were housed in the open surrounded by large moats and metal fences for the safety of the public.

We usually had a picnic on Dunstable Downs during this trip and watched the gliders taking off below us. It was a lovely serene enjoyable scene.

Chapter 14

War Memories at home.

It was September 1939 and once again there was a crisis and war was imminent.

Germany had invaded Poland and an ultimatum had been given with an 11am deadline on Sunday the 3rd of the month.

At that time, along with the rest of the nation I suppose, we turned on the radio to find out if Germany had withdrawn their troops but Mr Chamberlain's 11am announcement came over to say that there had been no answer to the ultimatum and that therefore we were at war with Germany. There was a shocked silence in the room, broken by my mother bursting into tears - after all, her generation had already suffered one war. My father put his arms round her and assured her that, at the age of 39, he was unlikely to be called into the Forces. He had served in the First World War.

I was worried by my mother's tears as she seldom cried and I was uncertain to know what to feel. The uncertainty was increased when, just a few minutes after the announcement, the air raid sirens sounded. The warning was soon followed by the steady note of the 'All Clear' but it was a bit of a fright for a second or two and it made me realise that we really were at war and German bombers could come over and drop bombs.

For a long time nothing warlike happened and it was called 'The Phoney War'. It was treated as a big joke when a lone German bomber dropped a bomb in a rural area in Scotland which killed a rabbit. This gave rise to a song about it

Run, rabbit, run, rabbit, run, run, run
Run, rabbit, run, rabbit, run, run, run
Bang, bang, Bang, bang! goes the farmer's gun
Run, rabbit, run, rabbit, run, run, run

Soon train loads of bewildered evacuee children arrived from London to escape from the expected air raids and all had to be found homes.

I was in the Girl Guides and, with others, helped the Billeting Officers with the children as they arrived at St James School, sometimes just trying to cheer them up and later going round with them to get them housed. It made a sad procession with a Billeting Officer at the head followed by a crocodile of tired little boys and girls attended by the Guides. We trailed round the streets depositing the children with householders. The Officer had a list of who could take a child or children according to the space available in their home so we just had to deposit the children in the appropriate houses. Some children were welcomed with open arms but some were far from welcome and it was so sad to leave children where they were so obviously not wanted. On one of the trips I was taken with a small boy who was the very last to be taken in. I was holding his hand and paying him special attention because of this but when he was eventually billeted the Officer took me on one side and advised me to have a good bath and scrub when I got home. The poor lad was suffering from impetigo. I didn't dare tell my mother.

We took in one evacuee, a girl of about 9 or 10 years old, called Joy. Unfortunately she didn't live up to her name but we treated her as one of the family and did our best to help her settle in. She was an only child and I suppose it must have been hard for her to be suddenly in a family of three children.

I well remember one day that Mum had to take Joy to the doctor. She had been complaining of earache but the doctor couldn't find any reason for it hurting. Mum was a little annoyed at a wasted visit which in those times had to be paid for, but she nearly exploded as we were walking home to hear Joy say, in a small voice, "Auntie, the doctor was looking in the wrong ear". Mum couldn't thump Joy so I got thumped for laughing.

Her family came to visit her most weekends and Mum always gave them a meal even though they never helped out with rationed food.

They brought sweets for Joy and after they had gone Joy would go off on her own. I thought she was upset at being left until I found out that she was going to the bottom of the garden to eat all her sweets. We had always been brought up to offer sweets round before starting to eat them ourselves so this greedy behaviour made me furious. I told her that she should at least have offered some to Brian but, again, as an only child she never had to share and couldn't understand why I was cross.

Apart from evacuees life went on much as usual at the beginning of the war. We had all been issued with Identity cards and gas masks which we had to carry everywhere.

During the war the News was avidly listened to and one of the daily bulletins was preceded by the playing of all the Allies National Anthems and a drum sounding the V (for Victory) dot dot dot dash. The announcers always said their names – Here is the 9 o clock news read by Alvar Liddel – so that we knew we were listening to a true bulletin and not one from an enemy station.

The 'Facts of Life' was a subject never mentioned by my mother. I had noticed that, during the news bulletins, figures of rising cases of VD were given out. Listening to these figures one evening curiosity got the better of me and I asked "What's VD Mum?" There was a horrified silence from Mum and Dad, and Geoff nearly choked on his food trying to hide his laughter. I got absolutely no answer, in fact it was as if I hadn't spoken. Mum had already let me start my first period knowing nothing at all about it. It doesn't need much imagination to know how she found out but after she had shown me how to deal with it she just said, "You know all about this don't you?". She was obviously embarrassed so I said I did but I didn't tell her that for days I had worried that something was terribly wrong with me. Because of this I thought that the VD question was just one more thing for me to find out for myself.

Northampton didn't suffer much from air raids. It was said that, because we were situated in a valley the Germans passed over us. Whether there was any truth in that we never knew but it was a comforting thought.

The first bombs fell in 1940 but no air raid warning sounded. I was in bed and could hear these funny 'crumping' noises in the distance. I didn't attach any importance to the noise and it never crossed my mind to go downstairs to ask Mum and Dad about it. It was a shock therefore when suddenly there was a very loud explosion and we all realized that bombs were dropping. Mum called upstairs for Brian and I to come down at once. There was a big window half way down our stairs and I suddenly froze, not wanting it to blow in on me. Geoff appeared, noticed my fright and gave me a shove from behind, telling me to get a move on. That got me moving again and we were quickly making for the shelter.

We found out the next day that the bombs had hit bungalows in Duston. The occupants were safe but a warden had mistaken a live, sparking electric cable for an incendiary bomb and used a stirrup pump to put it out. Unfortunately for him it was a high voltage cable so he was electrocuted and killed.

A crowd gathered and we all stood silently looking in awe at our first air raid damage and feeling so sorry for Northampton's first casualty.

For some reason the sirens never sounded before the bombs dropped so it was always a very hurried exit from our house, getting over the fence and into the Anderson shelter next door. On one memorable night my mother managed to get herself stuck getting over the fence and it took Dad pulling and Geoff pushing to get her free. Once in the shelter, which was quite cosy, the adults always made tea - they added whisky to theirs, to settle their nerves! I thought it smelled and tasted revolting. If the All

Clear was a long time coming and nothing was happening, we would go back to our house where Brian and I would spend the rest of the night on a makeshift bed under the stairs - reckoned to be the safest place in a bombed house, short of a direct hit of course.

We were told that you would never hear the bomb that hit you but surely I wasn't the only one who wondered how anyone would know that. If a victim was killed by a bomb it wouldn't be possible for him to say he didn't hear it

Although we couldn't have an Anderson shelter in our garden because it would have flooded we preferred to share our next door neighbour's rather than go to one of the three street shelters in our road. These were brick built, above ground and didn't look very strong. There was a deeper trench shelter on a grassy island on Spencer Bridge road that was covered by a large earth mound. This would have given more protection than the street shelters but I don't recall anyone using any of them. The one on the green was used for courting couples and all the shelters smelt as if they'd been used as toilets. I suppose if bombs were dropping and folk were out in the open the shelters would have been used.

Bombs were dropped elsewhere in Northamptonshire but never as an all out attack, more that the aircraft were dropping the last of their load as they headed for home. We soon got used to the sound of the German bombers, a very different engine noise to our own aircraft.

Brian and I spent all of one night under the stairs as waves of German bombers were going over. It was the night of November 14th 1940 and the planes went on to bomb Coventry. Huge fires were started first by incendiary bombs followed by massive destruction from the high explosive bombs. We could see the glow from the flames from our street. We were feeling so sorry for the unfortunate people who were suffering from this awful raid but, of course, we didn't know then that Coventry and its citizens were the victims of a vicious terror attack. The city centre was devastated by the fires and then the bombs and the cathedral was left as just a shell. The bombs had disrupted the water mains so the fires were soon out of control throughout the city and the bombers came over in waves until about 6 o clock the next morning.

Hundreds of people were killed and wounded, including firemen and other workers who were trying to rescue people trapped in the wreckage.

A new word came into our language, I think Churchill formed it when he visited after the raid and any other wide spread damage after that was said to be 'Coventrated'.

Much later on when we went over to the city to see for ourselves we saw that the priest had fashioned a cross out of two charred pieces of wood and put it where the altar used to be.

Geoff was working as a GPO telephone engineer at this time and the next morning he was sent with other emergency workers to restore communications. He never told us of the sights he saw over the following days but it was bad enough to put him off his food for a while, which was very rare for him as he loved his food.

I think it was because of this experience that, as soon as he was old enough, he volunteered for the RAF. He was in a reserved occupation so Mum and Dad must have thought that he was safe from military service. It was a shock for them when, one day, he came home and announced that he'd joined the RAF. Mum vanished into the kitchen to weep but we were all proud of him.

In 1940 Winston Churchill became Prime Minister in place of Mr Chamberlain. At this time the threat of German invasion was in the mind of everyone and we listened to Churchill's first speech on the radio when he said that he had nothing to offer us but 'blood, toil, tears and sweat' which I found a bit frightening. The speech that frightened me even more was when he said we would fight on the beaches,

Geoff in RAF uniform

in the fields and in the streets but we would never surrender. My vivid imagination could see German soldiers fighting in our Northampton street. I didn't know then that my mother's imagination was way ahead of mine and that she planned to kill me if the Germans came. I had the blonde hair and blue eyes of the Aryan race and she thought I would be taken away to have babies for Germany. She told me this many years after the war. However, she didn't tell me how she would have done it.

In 1941 a German bomber jettisoned the last of his bombs over Northampton. One landed in the Cemetery and exploded amongst the graves. No one was injured but there were many tales the next day of people claiming they had pieces of grave stones landing in their gardens, all of which were said to have had RIP on them. Not all of them could have been true!

My father joined the LDV (Local Defence Volunteers) later called the Home Guard and had to attend meetings. He later joined the AFS (Auxiliary Fire Service), I don't know why he changed but he really enjoyed the duties more. He had to train in the various duties of firemen but as Northampton was never a prime target of the German bombers, he was never called upon to attend incidents.

He had to report to the HQ when the sirens sounded an alert and I recall one such occasion during a Christmas party at Nan Ives. We, Mum, Brian and myself, decided to walk home past the Fire Station where Dad left us to report for duty. The clear night sky was lit by a full moon, called a Bombers Moon in those days, and this made us nervous as we could hear planes overhead. We got to a bridge over the railway line and were right on the top when an engine underneath let off steam. We all jumped violently at the sudden loud noise and broke into a run.

Railway engines tried to shelter under bridges during a raid to hide the glow of their boiler fires from any enemy planes. The railway carriages were blacked out.

We had to laugh at our reaction but we were glad to get home and to hear the All Clear siren a bit later.

Dad also took his turn with nightly fire watching at the bus depot where he worked. He told us that on one occasion he and his colleague thought a sudden hail storm had started only to realise that the hail stones were in fact machine gun bullets from a plane. They quickly dived for cover!

It was surprising that the depot was never bombed as half the premises had been taken over for aircraft building. The metal shutters were often left open and the Lancaster bombers were clearly visible from the main road in front of the yard.

It was during the war that concerts were held in Carnegie Hall in the Central Library. There was no charge and they were mostly piano recitals. These concerts were my introduction to the beautiful music of Chopin.

I used to go to the New Theatre in Northampton to concerts given by well known orchestras from London and other cities.

I could only afford seats up in the 'Gods' which were high up in the theatre which, as the seats couldn't be reserved, involved a lengthy wait in the queue. Only the head of the queue was under shelter so quite often the other people in the queue had to put up with the cold and damp.

Ballet companies came to Northampton so I queued up for these too and soon came to love the dancing and music. There were two or three performances in a week and I was quite envious of my brother Geoff as he could afford the better seats and could go to more than one performance.

I saw Coppelia for the first time but as the seats in the Gods were so high it was impossible to see the balcony scenes. It was many years after that I saw it in full.

Geoff and I both bought records of music from these performances. I usually went into town on a Saturday afternoon with a friend and we often went to Abel's music shop on the market square. This was a very popular shop as it was possible to ask to hear a record before buying. The assistant would then relay the music to one of several cubicles. I sampled many pieces in this way but it didn't always result in a purchase. If I was trying to buy a classical piece it was usually on three records as in those days the records were 12" vinyl and used both sides. If the piece was completed in two and a half records a shorter classical piece was used on the last side. I always felt that I was getting something for nothing. Another bonus was that it was possible to buy one record at a time to build up to the full piece.

Geoff had a portable record player and let me listen to my records on it but one day when he was out I wanted to listen to one of his, the Revolutionary Study by Chopin. Unfortunately I didn't put the lid up far enough to lock it and, to my horror, it fell down during the playing and pushed the needle to deeply scratch right across the record. I dreaded telling him what had happened when he came home and he was cross, rightly so, but wouldn't let me buy a replacement record.

One day he showed me a really funny thing with the player. He took a used matchstick, sharpened the end and split the sharpened end to form two prongs. He then took out the needle and replaced it with the matchstick so that when the record was played it was playing two grooves at once. We decided to play a Deanna Durbin record of 'The Maids of Cadiz' and the result was hilarious with her soprano voice trilling away seeming to sing a duet with herself. We both finished up in tears of laughter. I recently heard the piece again and it took me straight back to that afternoon.

Any old records or those I didn't want anymore I made into dishes. I would hold the edges in a gas flame until they became pliable so that I could turn them up and mould into a fluted design. The record label would then be at the bottom and become the centre decoration. The finished dishes looked quite pretty and I gave them as presents to the family. The 7 inch records could hold sweets and the 12 inch were suitable for fruit.

Another thing that springs to mind is the first time I visited my grandparents during the blackout I had what seemed a brilliant idea to find their house. They lived at Number 15 so, when I got to the first house, I started to count 1-3

5 until I got to 15. I fumbled my way into the house and along the dark

passage to the living room where I could hear voices. I carefully turned the door handle and burst into the room calling "Boo" I was met by what seemed a sea of shocked faces – I was in the wrong house. I shut the door and bolted.

I found out later that the numbers weren't in sequence. After that I found the right house by feeling the numbers.

I never heard what the occupants said but my family was highly amused

Chapter 15

War memories at school.

All school children had to return to their schools the following day or two. That was the end of my extended holiday which had been a perk for Grammar school pupils.

However, once back at school we were told that Kilburn Grammar School from London was to be evacuated 'en masse' and the girls were going to attend our school - we would be taught in the mornings, starting at 8.30 and finishing at about 1pm plus Saturday mornings and they would take over in the afternoons.

It was not a very easy situation as we had to share our form room desks. In those days we could leave most of our text and note books in our desks so that we would only have to carry the appropriate books to other class rooms or to take home for homework. Now we had to cram all our books into half the space which could be difficult if the girl sharing was untidy.

It took a while to get used to grammar school procedures. We had our form room but for some lessons we had to gather our books and go to special rooms which had apparatus, the science lab had Bunsen burners, the Art studio, high up in the building had easels and other equipment and, of course, the gym had the ropes, vaulting horse and climbing bars etc. When the end of a lesson bell sounded the school was filled with girls making their way to the different rooms. There were prefects at each of the stairways and in the corridors to make sure we kept to the right and didn't run.

The Hall had prints of famous paintings hung on all the walls to instill in us an appreciation of the artists' work. I believe that this was an idea of our Head Mistress, Miss Millburn and she gave a short talk about each painting in turn after morning Prayers. I specially liked some of the paintings by Van Gogh, notably his vase of sunflowers and a field of poppies. For some reason too I was drawn to his painting of a Yellow Chair. The paintings were changed at intervals but these remained my favourites.

Our forms were divided into scholarship and fee paying girls which made for a bit of snobbery. The scholarship forms were straightforward Form V and the fee paying classes were labeled Form V P (parallel). Although most of the fee paying girls looked down on us, they had a lower standard of work than us. It was on the whole though friendly rivalry.

Our English mistress introduced a form of snobbery when she included elocution. She sneered at the Northampton accent by making sentences including boil and oil. She then substituted bile and ile in the Northampton way. I had never noticed these differences until then and thought it didn't matter much to have a local accent.

One amusing example though was the tale of one of the kindergarten class telling that she was looking for Miss Hughes, her form mistress. In the local accent it came out as "I'm looking for me shoes" which caused some confusion.

We had a drill to follow in case of an air raid. On the signal we had to stand up at our desks, turn round, get under the desk and put the seat down over our heads.

We also had gas mask drills and had to put them on correctly. We had to put a piece of card over the intake and breathe in hard to test that no air was leaking in from round the edges of the mask. This was horrible but on a lighter note breathing out produced a rude sound which reduced most of us to giggles which of course made the noise even louder. We had to settle down and keep the masks on for part of the lesson. It was always a relief to be told we could take them off.

We had a mid-morning break at school when we streamed down to the music room. There was a hatch leading to the kitchen where we collected our free milk and bought doughnuts or iced buns to go with it. At first my favourite doughnuts had masses of jam in the middle and were thickly covered in sugar. As rationing took hold the jam got less and less and the sugar eventually vanished altogether. Likewise the iced buns were at first thickly iced with white or pink icing which got less until it was just a smear of icing. We took it all in our stride and I don't recall anyone moaning about it. I think that 'Don't you know there's a war on?' became the first catch phrase of the war.

Our Domestic Science lessons were badly affected by war time restrictions. We were still taught some cooking although a lot of the ingredients were rationed and our mothers' were reluctant to risk our cooking with them. There was a store cupboard in the room and we were allowed to use dried fruit from the tins in there. I'm afraid a lot of us yielded to temptation and took some to eat as well as to cook with. It must have been noticed but nothing was ever said.

Alternate terms were given to cooking and sewing but when clothing coupons were introduced our mothers' again were reluctant to use them for material to make dresses etc which were not really needed. Instead we had to practice our stitching and darning on spare pieces of material.

Later in the War school dinners were introduced. I believe it was both to help with the rationing at home and because a lot of mothers were now out all day doing war work. We had to go to the College of Technology which was next door to our school and although the food was awful we enjoyed mixing with the students as we queued for our meal.

Opposite our school was a big park called the Racecourse and half of it was given over to an Army camp. The path through this part ran alongside the camp and the soldiers quite often lined the fence to call out to the girls on their way to and from school. They were mostly Czech I believe and I suppose it cheered them a bit as they were a long way from home. However, a girl in my form became a little too friendly with a soldier and when she fainted at school the visiting school nurse found that she was pregnant. She promptly vanished from our midst and never came back to school after that. We never heard about what happened to her but needless to say once the news of her pregnancy was passed round the school it caused quite a stir.

We were given very sketchy sex education at school and on one occasion a film was shown. Before it was projected we were told that it was a serious topic and on no account should we giggle. We didn't but we soon noticed that some of the form mistresses were hiding their giggles behind their hands. I think the films embarrassed them more than us

We got used to sharing our school with the evacuee pupils of Kilburn Grammar and found a lot of them very friendly. They invited us to go to their Youth Club which was a novelty for our single sex school status and we enjoyed the mixing with both the girls and the boys. The Club was held after school and after a while a very nice boy took to seeing me safely home. We enjoyed each others company and only met at the Club, a bit tame by today's standards I suppose. However, towards the end of the war and the air raids had eased, a lot of the pupils went back to London. It's a great shame that I can't remember his name as when he got home we started to write to each other. After a while I got a sad letter from him to say that his parents had ordered him to stop writing to me. He was Jewish and was only supposed to be friendly with Jewish girls. I had no idea that he was a Jew and thought it a shame to have to cease our letter writing. My first taste of racism!

A lot of friendships were formed and eventually our Head Mistress requested that the boys met the girls away from the school as she didn't approve of a crowd of boys at the school gates.

Every morning at school started with prayers, hymns and announcements in the Hall and everyone attended. The hall was overlooked by an upstairs balcony and the Catholics and other religions had to be there so they would hear any announcements but wouldn't join in the C of E prayers. The prayers always included asking for the safety of our Forces and the hymns were often for them too. We sang Eternal Father Strong to Save, O God Our Help in Ages Past, Onward Christian Soldiers and the like.

Our Head Mistress gave us a talk each morning and if she touched on the War, she told us we should pray for the Germans too. This theme occurred on several mornings and it got to the ears of some parents who were incensed by her pro German talk. In the end she was told she must stop. This information spread round the school like wildfire and we were never told to love our enemies again.

Our Music mistress, Miss Ewings, was at the piano and at the end of the assembly we were marched out to her stirring marches. In our music lessons she taught us how to sing the hymns and she was very particular on our pronunciation, especially the word Alleluluia, it had to be **Ar**le-- and not **Ally**--. We also had to sing O Come All Ye Faithful in Latin.

Miss Ewings really awoke my interest and enjoyment of music as part of her lesson was spent listening to records of classical pieces. I particularly remember her playing Nimrod, part of Elgar's Enigma Variations. She first of all explained that there were several examples of 'the fall of the eighth' in the piece and asked us to count how many there were. I was quite proud when I was the only one in the class to get the correct number.

I was so keen on music that one wet day when we had to spend our break indoors, I sat down at the piano in the Hall and told the group round it that I would play for them Tchaikovski's piano concerto in B flat. The start of the concerto starts with octaves ranging from the bass, middle and treble. Of course I had no idea of how to play them properly so I just plonked down the keys in the appropriate places and then sang the melody at the top of my voice. We all collapsed laughing and when I looked up I saw that two of the Mistresses were laughing with us.

My next venture into making music didn't have the same ending. Our Science Mistress was Miss Tranter and when she left the Lab we were supposed to occupy ourselves in her absence. We were quickly bored so I persuaded the class to get out combs and paper and then I sat up on the front bench to conduct them in playing tunes. As I was on that bench it meant that my back was to the door and after a while my 'orchestra' started to dwindle in confusion leaving me playing on my own. I turned round and found that Miss Tranter had returned and was waiting for me to stop. She was quite calm about it but I was banished to the Hall for the rest of the lesson. She didn't give me the ultimate punishment, a visit to the Head Mistress. Maybe she realized that no one was afraid of that. It was far worse to be spotted by Miss Webb, the school Secretary, and have to tell her of your wrong doing. She was quite frightening and would deliver a very stern lecture. Luckily she didn't spot me out in the Hall during the lesson.

As I've said previously, when the air raids over London eased, a lot of the pupils went back home and our school hours changed to include some afternoons in the week. We found this a bit hard as we had got used to having our afternoons free.

I loved the cinema and went as often as my pocket money allowed. One week I was dismayed to find that the Savoy cinema was showing the much vaunted film 'Gone With The Wind'. It was a very long film and as I had to be home by 9pm if I went out in the evening, I would miss a large part of the film. A school friend was also keen to see it so we decided to skip school one day and go to the matinee. Neither of us had done this before so we were quite nervous in case we were spotted. We crept to our seats and as the programme hadn't started, the lights were still on. We were even more nervous at this and slid down in our seats so that we couldn't be seen by anyone behind us. We were very much relieved when at last the lights dimmed and the film started. I have to say that in spite of all the apprehension we still enjoyed the film and felt it was well worth it although we never did it again.

On two other occasions I managed to get some time away from school with a fairly valid reason. My friend Thelma broke her arm but came back to school after a while. When she had to go back to the hospital to have the plaster removed it was decided that someone should go with her. I'm not sure if she asked for me or if I volunteered but I accompanied her to Casualty one morning and we gave ourselves the rest of the day off.

The other occasion a friend, Vera, was called home one morning because of rising flood water in St James, a regular occurrence, Our Form mistress asked if anyone else lived in that area and, of course, I put my hand up and joined Vera to catch the bus home. The flood water had reached the main road near her house but she managed to get home. I stayed on the bus which managed to get through the flood to my stop. Although our house didn't get flooded, the water came half way up the garden.

We practised another trick, this time to get away from school early. Our French mistress was deaf so when French was the last lesson of the day someone would raise their hand to tell her "La cloche est sonée Madame".

We found another time waster, this time in the History period. Our Mistress thought we should be knowledgeable in the progress of the War so she started each lesson with current affairs. She invited us to ask questions and of course we took advantage of that and the questions often lasted for the whole lesson. Usually she would realise that the lesson was nearly over and she then dictated passages from the actual lesson time, to try to follow the syllabus for forthcoming exams. It was not the best way to learn history but we brought it on ourselves.

In one of her lessons one girl made a flippant remark about fighting in the 1914-1918 War. I can't remember what is was but Miss H seemed to get very upset about it and dashed out of the class room. We were all shocked by this reaction and made a guess that she lost a relative or boyfriend during that time.

We couldn't waste time in the Latin periods as our Mistress for that was a Scottish lady who seemed to hate her pupils. She was usually late and bustled in, throwing her case on the table and growling out a greeting in Latin to which we had to reply also in Latin. Her case was hurled with such venom that it often slid across the table on to the floor. None of us dared to laugh or even to smile. It was difficult and if anyone failed to hide her mirth, Miss McKay came down on her like a ton of bricks. Her favourite put down remarks were all variations of a theme, saying that if we were examples of 'The Brave New World' the world was going to be in a sorry state.

The lessons were mainly with reading and translating English to Latin and Latin to English. At the beginning of the lesson we had to write the date on the blackboard. I was first up to write it on the Ides of March – 15th March, my birthday but I can't remember any other date!

I was wrong in deciding Latin was a useless lesson as I found much later on in life that it's quite a help with spellings and derivations of words in other languages, even though our Latin must have been taught with a Scottish accent.

My very favourite lessons were gym and games taken by a Miss D who was in the habit of addressing us by our surnames and generally regimenting us. If any girl found favour with her she would start to call her by her Christian name. I was one of those girls but I didn't know at once. It was only when she called out to me by the name Patricia, my real name. She said 'Don't you know your name girl?' and jabbed her finger at me so I had to explain that I was always called Molly. She thought it was a bit strange but she always called me Molly after that.

The gym at NSG

I had a mishap in one gym lesson. We were divided into groups of three and two of us had to help the third to turn a somersault between two ropes. Miss D told us not to stand in front of the third girl if she was having difficulties doing it but we had the tallest and heaviest girl to help and I forgot the warning and could only heave her up by standing a bit in front. To make things worse I had a habit of biting on my lip when exerting myself so when her knees came up to start the somersault, they hit me under the chin and drove my teeth right through my lip. The blood poured out, over my blouse and onto the floor. Miss D rushed me up to the first aid point in the gym and put pressure on my lip with a dressing. She then asked me if I was alright and when I politely said 'Yes thank you', the dressing came off and the blood flowed again. The only thing different was that we both couldn't stop laughing.

On a lighter note I learned to play tennis and hockey and with her extremely efficient coaching managed to reach a good standard. I also did well in swimming and took part in the Galas. It was Miss D who taught me the racing dive which I mentioned in an earlier chapter.

We held our annual Sports Days when parents were invited to attend. Mine never did and, in fact, they never attended any other functions. However I always enjoyed Sports Days All pupils were divided into 'Houses' in their first days at the School, and our uniforms showed which was which by incorporating their house colours, Clare, (red), Dryden (yellow), Elwes (blue) and Washington (green). I was in Clare so my tie had red stripes.

This made all Sports Days, tennis matches, hockey matches and swimming galas extremely competitive. Clare usually did well so I was pleased to be part of it.

I had a very nasty experience during my first year at the School. I had been suffering from an itchy scalp and then got a rash on the back of my neck. I was complaining about it to Mum and she had a look at it. To my horror, and hers, she found that I had head lice and the rash was actually bites from them. Geoff was in the room at the time and his reaction was "Ugh, don't come near me!" At that I burst into tears and said 'that's what everyone will say'. Mum was more than horrified, she was livid and the next day she was at the school declaring that she didn't expect this sort of thing to happen in a school like mine. I was off school for that day at least and I was treated with the awful remedy of first covering my head with paraffin oil, leaving it for what seemed hours and then swilling it with vinegar. After that it was a session of sitting in a chair with a newspaper on my lap while Mum combed through my hair with a nit comb. I don't know which was worse, the smell or seeing the dead lice and nits fall onto the paper. I was persuaded to go back to school the next day and I felt that everyone could smell the vinegar. Mum had been promised that no one would mention it but someone had passed it on so I suppose it should have been told. It took a lot of sessions of the treatment before Mum was satisfied that my head was clear of lice and nits and the whole episode was horrific. I think Geoff felt guilty about his reaction as he was very nice to me afterwards. He was probably sorry for upsetting me about it.

Thank goodness that nowadays the treatment is very quick and there is no stigma attached to infestation as it's known that the lice only pick on clean heads.

Some time during 1942 all children were injected with an antitoxin to protect them against diphtheria. When it was available for our school we all had to line up in the Hall with our arms bared ready for the injection. I wasn't happy about this at all and protested that I didn't need the injection as I had already had diphtheria. No one took a bit of notice and when my turn came, the needle went in.

I'm glad that due to these precautions cases of the illness are now very rare but nevertheless, when my two daughters were born in 1951 and 1955 I was very prompt in taking them to our GP for their injections. He was a bit puzzled by my urgency but when I explained my own experience of the disease he understood and told me that he had never seen a case of diphtheria during his training or his following career.

I used to take the bus to school most of the time but it meant changing buses at Town Centre and if I missed a connection it made me late. I also found the walk over the Racecourse a bit tedious so I used to take my roller skates with me and skate across instead. Luckily I was never spotted by any of the mistresses as I'm sure they wouldn't have approved of such 'unladylike' behaviour.

I soon found it was more convenient to cycle and quite enjoyed it although I remember one day cycling with tears streaming down my face. I had just found out that Geoff was going to America to train as a pilot and I felt that all the U boats in the Atlantic would be trying to sink his boat.

Another time I was walking with Daphne and pushing my cycle. I had had a Toni home perm which had left my hair so curly that I couldn't get my school hat on properly so it was on the front of the bike. I saw two mistresses coming towards us and thought it wasn't much use cramming my hat on as they must have noticed I wasn't wearing it. Sure enough they stopped me and asked why I was not wearing my hat but they had to laugh when I demonstrated that it wouldn't fit over my curls. They insisted that I try so I managed to get it on and wore it until they were out of sight.

I have to admit though that the hat was usually on the front of my bike more often than on my head.

My best friend at that time was Daphne B who developed a crush on a shop assistant called Maurice. She persuaded me to travel by bus again and to get off at the bus stop near to her house so that we could walk past the shop on the way to school. She always hoped he would be sweeping the path outside the shop as we passed but if he wasn't she would go slowly past and pretend to be admiring the window display. She was actually looking into the shop and admiring him. I often wondered if he noticed.

This stopped after a while as she had to leave school when she was 15 years old. Her mother was a widow and told the Education Authority that she needed Daphne to get a job and bring in a wage. On awarding scholarships a condition was that parents had to sign an agreement to keep pupils at school until the age of 16 but exceptions were made in cases of hardship.

One day at Morning Prayers, a few weeks before we broke up for the long summer holiday, Miss Millburn announced that a lady wanted a girl to look after her daughter during the afternoons of our holiday. My friend Daphne and I were attracted by this and saw Miss Millburn afterwards for more details. We had an interview with the mother and, as we were the only applicants, she arranged with us to go on alternate days. Daphne quickly lost interest so I went every week day.

When I arrived for the first day I found it was assumed that I also had to look after a Downs Syndrome girl. This was taking advantage of me as there had been no mention of this until I actually got there. I had never had any contact with Downs Syndrome, in those days they were called Mongols, but she seemed to be a happy girl and was easier to manage than the first girl. I think they must have been sisters but I had no explanation of her connection with the family.

I was supposed to teach the girl reading and arithmetic but she didn't want to have any lessons. The Downs girl really wanted to learn to read but her 'sister' was scornful of any attempts she made. She really was an unpleasant child, about five years old but arrogant, rude and I suspect very spoilt. By contrast the little Downs girl who looked older was very eager to please and chattered away quite happily. I became very fond of her.

The lessons were in the first half of the afternoon and for the second half their mother wanted them to be taken out on walks. I usually took them to Abington Park as this was quite close to their home and they enjoyed the playground there and going down to the lake to see the swans and ducks.

I was glad to get to the end of the afternoon, mostly because of the younger child's behaviour. I suppose she saw me as a servant and certainly, at times, spoke to me in that manner.

I looked after them for most of the holiday and then made my excuses and left.

Towards the beginning of our Christmas holiday another job was announced by Miss Millburn. The GPO needed extra staff for the busy Christmas post. This time there were several of us interested and in due course we were taken on.

We had quick tuition on how the post was sorted, all by hand in those days. I was put to sorting post into the pigeon holes of the different streets in Northampton. From time to time a post man would reach over my shoulder to collect the mail for his delivery round or 'walk' as I believe they called it. Another post man would bring the piles of mail to different points to be sorted. I really enjoyed this and tried to see how fast I could get through each batch brought to me. Sometimes I would finish before the next batch arrived and at one time we temps were asked to slow down a bit so as not to upset the regulars.

In the last week before Christmas the Mayoral party came round the Sorting Office to be shown how the mail was dealt with. This was just one of their Christmas visits in the town. They also visited Hospitals and Homes. They still do the rounds now but I haven't seen photos of visits to the Royal Mail for a long time.

I was quite sorry when we finished but managed to make another Christmas session before I left school. We were paid for this work which was a great help with my Christmas shopping.

Chapter 16

Cinema and Theatre

Northampton had many cinemas, about a dozen, in their heyday and I started my cinema visits with the Rink in St James. It was always called the Rink when I was young as the building started as a skating rink and it was many years after, that it rejoiced in the name of The Roxy.

I was allowed to go to the Saturday matinees from quite a young age but I had to go with Geoff who hated to have a young sister in tow. He walked with me until we turned the corner out of Mum's sight and then picked up speed so that I had a job to keep up with him. I was therefore a couple of steps behind him which saved his pride. We always managed to arrive home together so Mum never guessed that we parted company at the cinema.

The front entrance to the cinema was on the Main Road but for the matinee we had to queue at the side door in St James Park Road. When the doors opened a man stood at the entrance with a cloth bag to collect our 2 pennies to go in. It was called the Twopenny (Tuppny) Rush because it was always a crush to get in first. Those lucky enough to be at the front were able to get the best seats. Sometimes children, always boys, boasted that they had only put 1 penny in the bag. If you had more money you could go in at the front for 6d and have the very best seats.

Once the show started we were treated to a serial, usually a cowboy, and a 'big' film starring The Three Stooges, Laurel & Hardy, Lucan & McShane or George Formby. I didn't like Lucan & McShane, or Old Mother Riley and her daughter Kitty as their act was called.

It was a bit rowdy as if the boys (again) had any comments about the films they shouted them out. I don't recall the girls doing this.

When I was a bit older Mum let me go to the Majestic which was nearer to the town centre. It was more expensive but had better films.

The main cinemas in town were the Exchange and the Savoy. The Exchange was on a higher level from the street and the queues for the childrens' shows stretched down many stairs and outside along the side of the Market Square. It was funny at the end of the performances as if we'd seen a cowboy film the boys would come down the stairs swaggering like the film stars and if it was a film with a lot of dancing the girls would emerge, not quite dancing but very light footed.

Both of these cinemas were big so that even if you were far back in the queue you could usually get a seat. A uniformed usher controlled the queues and made sure nobody pushed in ahead of their place.

Both the Exchange and the Savoy had an organ although there was not always an organist at the Exchange. During the interval the organ would come from the pit up to stage level and popular melodies would be played while usherettes sold ice creams at the sides of the auditorium. The Savoy had a Compton organ with lighted panels at each side which changed colours.

Between the B movie and the main film there were other features.

During the war the Newsreels were the most important as during the war everyone was keen to see news of battles and air raids on Germany as well as home news. Any bad news was lightly touched on and all was biased so as to keep up the morale of the public.

There were war films too and two I particularly remember. One was called 'One Of Our Aircraft Is Missing'. It featured a bomber which had the call sign F for Freddie and showed the briefing, the actual bombing raid over Germany and the tension of the Operation Room waiting to see if any aircraft were missing. F for Freddie was shot down and the crew was helped by the Dutch Underground to get back to England.

The other was Dangerous Moonlight and starred Anton Walbrook as a Polish pianist and later a pilot. The theme music was the Warsaw Concerto and the shot which has stayed in my memory was when Anton Walbrook was escaping to England in a plane and as he flew over Warsaw he was looking from his plane to view the widespread bomb damage.

Both these films were, of course, propaganda as were others made in that time.

There was another cinema in Town Centre, the Temperance, usually called the Temp. It was known locally as The Flea Pit and as the name suggests it was very shabby with damaged, dusty seats and grubby décor. I believe it was the oldest cinema in Northampton. I only went there a few times and only if they were showing a film I really wanted to see.

Among the other cinemas in or near town were three others the Ritz, Tivoli and Plaza owned and managed by two brothers, Sydney and Myer Cipin. They ruled with a rod of iron and wouldn't tolerate any rowdyism.

These smaller cinemas usually had twice weekly programmes, Monday to Wednesday and Thursday to Saturday. They had no upper circle seating whereas the larger cinemas had and these were more expensive than the lower seats.

Another cinema was The Regal and this too was a bit shabby but it had double seats at the back making it popular with courting couples.

Of course there was no air conditioning in those early days and in the summer it did get a bit stuffy. I suppose this was the reason that the usherettes went up and down the aisles with a perfumed spray.

It was a bit difficult for me to go to the cinemas in the outskirts of town as I had to be home by 9.30 pm. The programmes were continuous so if I went early I would see the end of the main feature film in the first house and then see the other part in the second house before leaving to get home in time. It spoilt some films, especially those with a surprise ending but I had to keep to the rules or forfeit any other visits for a time.

I was absolutely forbidden to walk home the quickest way. This took me through a seedy part of town which had a pub on each corner and Mum didn't think it safe for me to be there alone. I was alone as unfortunately none of my cinema going friends lived in St James.

I have to admit that if I was a bit late leaving the cinema I broke the rule but I didn't walk, I ran, very fast! This way was quicker than going to Town Centre to get a bus.

When I was young I was always taken to the two theatres in town to see the Pantomimes. The Repertory Theatre show was the best as they always stuck to the story. Of course there was interaction between the players and audience and singing. The actors started the songs and a large sheet was brought down onto the stage that had the words of the song written on it. Then it was the turn of the audience to sing and a small light danced over each word to help us. It was all good fun.

We went to the New Theatre but it was more of a variety show with the story too spaced out. As the years went by it got harder to identify the tale as it was interrupted by the 'stars' doing a comedy act. The jokes went from slightly suggestive to downright smutty and eventually we gave up going.

My parents took me to other shows at the theatre and I remember going to see Bertram Mills circus. It seemed a bit strange to have a circus in a theatre instead of a Big Top at an open air site. We did go to the more traditional tented site as well, which was at Midsummer Meadow

There were the usual juggling, high wire acts etc but the act that really intrigued me was the Giraffe-necked women. They wore many brass coils round their necks which looked extremely uncomfortable but as they had their first coils put on in childhood maybe they just took them for granted. They certainly looked very elegant.

I was taken to see the elephant's parade from the railway station to their stables and I loved how they walked, each holding the tail of the elephant in front.

When the circus was held at the Midsummer Meadow site they had a menagerie in another tent. Although I loved to see the animals I didn't like to see them cooped up.

Chapter 17

Radio

During the war the News was avidly listened to, one of the daily bulletins was preceded by the playing of all the Allies National Anthems and a drum sounding the V (for Victory) dot dot dot dash. The announcers always said their names – Here is the 9 o clock news read by Alvar Liddel – so that we knew we were listening to a true bulletin. not one from an enemy station.

The traitor, Lord Haw Haw, also broadcast news bulletins designed to lower our morale. He always started by announcing in a nasal voice "Germany calling, Germany calling" which sounded like Jarmany calling It was illegal to listen to him but he actually became quite popular with most of British listeners who were amused by his broadcasts. Occasionally he caused alarm by broadcasting accurate details passed on by Fifth Columnists (spies) but on the whole he wasn't taken seriously.

At the end of the war in Europe he was caught and executed for treason as, although he took German nationality, he still held a British passport.

From all accounts he was defiant to the end.

We had our favourite programmes, In Town Tonight was one. Eric Coates Knightsbridge March introduced it and after a few bars a voice could be heard in the background, getting louder and calling like a newspaper vendor ' In Town Tonight' followed by the announcer calling Stop and saying "Once more we stop the roar of the traffic to bring you some of the interesting people who are In Town Tonight. There followed indoor and outdoor interviews of the various guests which were usually very interesting. This programme started at the beginning of the war and went out early Saturday evenings.

Later on Saturday evenings, during the winters a series of plays called An Appointment with Fear were broadcast, introduced by Valentine Dyall known as The Man in Black. We would turn out the lights and listen to the thrillers by firelight. Valentine Dyall had a very deep voice which heightened the tension. His voice followed by the plays usually scared me. However I always listened but when it was finished, usually with a macabre twist, I quickly scampered upstairs to burrow under the bed clothes.

A popular pre-war programme was Bandwaggon with Arthur Askey and Richard Murdoch as the Stars. The plot had them living in the top floor flat of the BBC and their charwoman was Mrs Bagwash.

Part of the show was given over to Syd Walker as a rag and bone man. His signature tune was

Day after day
I'm on my way
Any rags, bottles or bones

He then told tales of various predicaments and asked people to advise him with the phrase

What would you do chums?

Listeners, including me, were very sorry when the show ended not long after the start of the war.

I believe that Richard Murdoch joined the RAF but he later starred with Kenneth Horne in Much Binding in the Marsh, the name of a fictitious RAF station

There were other favourite programmes to listen to and I suppose the most popular was ITMA – It's That Man Again – with Tommy Handley. It consisted of several sketches poking fun at wartime conditions. Lord Haw Haw became Fumf in one of them and began the sketch by announcing, This is Fumf Speaking, a phrase that was much repeated by the public

When my brother, Geoff, was home on leave from the RAF we quite often stayed up late chatting after Mum, Dad and of course Brian had gone to bed and we usually tuned in to a radio station called AFN (American Forces Network) Munich, Stuttgart.

This was broadcast as the Americans advanced through Germany but before then Geoff happened on some exciting news.

He used to listen to news sent by Morse code and one evening I was reading whilst he was tuned in to such a bulletin. He suddenly got very excited and said "It's started" and when I asked what had started and he replied "The Invasion". Naturally we were elated to know that the promised Second Front had begun and we debated whether or not to wake Mum and Dad to tell them the news. We decided against it but it took us a while to calm down. We sat talking about it for a long while and found it a sobering thought to realise there would be many men killed or wounded in the attack. Surprisingly we never had any doubts about it failing.

The news was given out on the early news bulletins and it was strange to think we were amongst the first to know about it.

Chapter 18

More visits

I spent some of my holidays with Aunt Helen & Uncle Bert in Leicester. I'm not sure how it came about but I don't think it was my idea as I didn't feel comfortable with them. Uncle Bert was strange as when I was there during the war years and was working at the GPO he showed too much interest in how the air raid warnings were routed through Northampton Telephone Exchange. I managed to give a non specific answer but he raised the questions several times and it was a while before he gave up. I was disconcerted too when I noticed that the insides of his envelopes were printed maps.

He wasn't pleased when I teased him about his surname, Gruber and Hitler's name of Schickelgruber!

When I was younger I found that the best thing about staying there was that they had a very nice lodger who owned a knitting and embroidery shop and she let me go with her to help(?) One of my favourite things was tidying the embroidery silks cabinet for her. She knitted a lovely set of clothes in pink for my baby doll. It consisted of a dress in a pretty lacy pattern, pants as well as a coat and bonnet.

After work she and Aunt Helen taught me embroidery stitches and showed me how to iron transfers on to material. I was quite disappointed at a later date when I found she had moved away from Leicester.

Aunt Helen did her best to amuse me and we had some pleasant walks in Bradgate Park. I was very interested to see the ruins of Bradgate House, the birthplace of Lady Jane Grey. I found her story so sad, being Queen for just 9 days and her eventual execution at the age of only 17.

I was still at school when I spent some of my holiday with relatives in Tipton and Coseley, W. Midlands.

Again I'm not sure how this happened or even how I got there but first I was with Harry, my mother's cousin, and and his wife, Dora in Tipton. Their address was Ocker Hill which was always called Ocker Bonk by the locals. They had a daughter called Hilda who was very much under her mother's thumb. Years later I learned she once had a steady boyfriend but when he was invited home Dora never spoke to him but just sat and stared at him making him thoroughly uncomfortable. Eventually he faded out of the picture and Hilda remained unmarried.

I used to think that Harry was good fun but he went down drastically in my estimation one wet day. The rain had stopped but their little back garden had attracted scores of frogs. To my horror Harry picked them up, one by one, threw them in the air and hit them with a flat piece of wood, as you might serve a tennis ball, to the bottom of the garden. He thought it was great fun but I was sickened.

During my visit I was taken to see Harry's parents, Alice and Harry who lived near the top of the road. Their house was very old fashioned and their lavatory was a privy in a dark shed at the bottom of the garden. I managed to give that a miss!

My mother had told me the story of when she was staying with them and needed the toilet. While she was sitting there she patted and was talking to what she thought was Aunt Alice's cat only to find, on opening the door, she had been making a fuss of a rat.

I was glad to be passed on to spend time with Hilda, another cousin, and Syd. They lived in a modern house in Coseley which was near to fields. Hilda was Syd's second wife and they had a son called Trevor who was older than me. He took me to play cricket with his friends in the field, which I enjoyed a lot but came to grief when I was put as wicket keeper. Trevor was batting and he swung his bat with all his strength, missed the ball and hit me in the face with his bat. He was horrified and terrified his parents would be very cross. He asked me not to tell, which I wouldn't have done, and we became even better friends because of that and we even enjoyed more games of cricket.

My favourite visits were to Aunt Norah and Uncle Ben who lived in Newport, Essex. When I was really young Mum and Dad took me for a day but when I got to be about nine I was allowed to travel alone - not something a child could do nowadays. The journey involved catching a bus from Northampton to Bedford, then changing to another bus to get to Cambridge. I used to get off the bus near the railway station to be met by Aunt Norah and then we would catch the train to Audley End. From there we would walk to her house at Carnation Cottages going through a farm yard. A gaggle of geese had the run of this yard and I always hoped they wouldn't see us. Of course they did and they started to cackle fiercely and chase after us. Aunt Norah used to say 'Don't run, don't run' but I had to use all my will power not to as every fibre of me wanted to run for my life.

I was always relieved to get through the yard to continue the walk through the fields to Aunt Norah's house on the outskirts of Newport.

Aunt Norah's cottage in Newport, Essex

The days were always busy in Newport and most of the time was spent in the open air. My first chore was to visit the three hen houses at the bottom of the garden to let the hens out and to collect the eggs - I disturbed many a hen, feeling underneath them in my eagerness to get those lovely warm eggs and I was always more pleased with the brown ones! The other enjoyable job with the hens was helping to mix their food and then filling the troughs and of course it was always good fun in the evening shooing them all back inside and shutting them in safely for the night.

I was always keen to run errands for Auntie as I loved to get into the village, and one regular trip took me to a garage right at the other end. As there was no electricity at the cottage the 'wireless' had to be run from an accumulator. This had to be taken to the garage to be re-charged. I therefore had to take the used one and exchange it for the freshly charged one. I enjoyed the walk but I was a little nervous about carrying the accumulator as it was mainly a glass box type container filled, I was told, with acid. It had some sort of connectors on top and also a carrying handle which I gripped firmly as my chief worry was that the acid would spill over or, worse still, I might drop it. The only thing I knew about acid was that it burns and I viewed the whole contraption as something of a booby-trap!

Aunt Norah always took me out either mornings or afternoons and we usually took the path over the fields to the village. We started by crossing the railway line at the bottom of her garden and then following the footpath into the middle of the village. On the way, according to the season, we would pick mushrooms, various nuts and blackberries. There was one field alongside our path from the railway line that we couldn't go in, which was quite frustrating as the best mushrooms were in there.

The other two main pickings were elderberries and, best of all, the gleanings of corn from one of the fields. We would go round the edge of the field to pick up what was missed by the reapers. I would roll the heads in my hands, blow away the husks to leave the lovely golden corn. This of course was for the chickens and we always got lots as the reapers were not as efficient as the modern combine harvesters.

While I was out amusing myself Auntie would be working in the house but I liked to come back to help her with the ironing. She used flat irons heated on the gas ring, one heating while she was using the other. She armed me with a thick cloth so that I could change them over for her and it always amused me to see her spit on the iron to test the heat before applying it to the freshly washed linen.

The evenings at Carnation Cottage were very cosy with the gas light and Auntie and I would knit while listening to the wireless. Sometimes Auntie and Uncle Ben would get out the cards and play 'Snap' or 'Draw the Well Dry' with me.

When it was time for bed I washed with collected rain water from the huge tank outside. Tap water was for drinking and domestic use. After milk and biscuits it was off to bed with a candle to light my way.

Another visit to Newport was sad. Uncle Ben was extremely ill and in a bed downstairs as he couldn't manage the stairs up to his bedroom. It was a very subdued visit and Mum and Dad tried to cheer up Aunt Norah. She asked them if they thought he would get well again and they replied 'Of course he will'. When we left in the car I heard Dad say to Mum that he didn't think Uncle Ben was going to get over his illness. I was already upset at seeing Uncle Ben so ill and Aunt Norah so upset that when I overheard Dad's remark I burst out that he'd told Aunt Norah a lie and he was awful to do that. I understood when I was older of course why they had said it but at the time they were too shocked at my outburst to explain. It was not long after that Uncle Ben died,

Chapter 19

Leaving School, starting Work

During my last year at school the pressure of the School Certificate began to mount with most of the mistresses reminding us of the need to concentrate to complete the syllabus. I was getting more and more stressed and hated the exams leading up to it.

For the School Certificate pupils had to pass in every subject taken. If this wasn't achieved all the subjects had to be taken again and not just the one or more the pupil had failed to pass. I didn't feel I had any chance of gaining the Certificate and felt depressed at the thought of even trying. One of the compulsory subjects was Maths and I knew I'd never pass in that.

I couldn't leave school until I was sixteen, an undertaking my parents had to sign when I won the Scholarship. My birthday was in March so if I could leave at Easter I could avoid the exam. I thought that if I could get a job my parents, and the school, would have no objection to me leaving.

I had always liked the idea of working with animals so, without telling my parents, I wrote to a local veterinary practice to ask for a job of a veterinary nurse. I had a very nice reply asking me to make an appointment for an interview but because of my secrecy I lost my nerve and didn't follow it up.

My brother, Geoff, had worked as a GPO Engineer before enlisting in the RAF and he had taken me to see both the engineering side and the Telephone Exchange switch room. I thought at the time that working as a telephone operator would be very interesting so I decided that I would apply for a post.

Again I had a nice reply with an appointment to attend for an interview and this time I told my parents what I had done. I also confessed my doubts about passing the School Cert and how worried I was about taking the exams. They understood and agreed that I should attend the appointment at the GPO. I think it helped that Geoff had been working and doing well there. So one afternoon, feeling a bit nervous, I presented myself at the Head Office to be interviewed. I knew that usually a School Certificate was required so again I had to be honest and say that I didn't think I could obtain one and hoped they would accept me without it. I had some voice and hearing tests and had to answer a lot of questions about my schooling etc. after which they thanked me for attending and said they would let me know. They didn't keep me waiting long and I had another letter with a request to go back. They then told me that my Head Mistress had said some very nice things about me and offered me the post with a starting date.

I was so happy and felt the weight of worry about the exam lifted from my shoulders. Mum and Dad were pleased for me too and wrote to the school asking for my release.

Things moved fairly quickly after that and I left school at Easter in time for me to take up my post in April 1944.

During my last week at school I played a hockey game which had gone well and we made our way back to the cloakroom in high spirits. One of the girls started playing around with her hockey stick and somehow got it tangled in my legs. I went down with a crash and landed heavily with my face hitting the tarmac drive. I lost all feeling round my nose and mouth but could tell by the others' faces that I'd done some damage. They wouldn't answer my pleas of 'What have I done?' but when I got to a mirror I could see why they were shocked. I was more shocked than they were when I saw my face was bleeding from grazing all round the bottom part of my face which was also beginning to swell from the bruising. Worse still, one of my front teeth was broken. I could hardly believe that this had happened almost on my last day at school and just a few days before I was due to start work!

There was nothing I could do about it and I duly presented myself at the Telephone Exchange with a swollen, grazed and badly bruised nose and mouth plus an aching half tooth. I looked an awful sight but by this time I had started to see the funny side of it and could laugh at the reaction I caused.

I joined a class of trainee telephonists and met our teacher, Miss Sheila T who would be in charge of us for eight weeks. The first thing we noticed was that we were addressed by our surnames although Miss T gave me the nickname of Nellie, I've no idea why.

The first thing she taught us was the standard expressions to use and never deviate from to the subscribers, even if they wanted friendly chat.

Funnily enough, although we were called Hello girls, Hello was a word we were not allowed to use.

I had all this so much in mind that one day, going home on the bus, I gave the conductor my fare, looked up into his face and said 'Number Please' I was so embarrassed but he either didn't realise what I'd said or chose to ignore it.

Each exchange, local and the main long distant places, had a code so that was another thing to learn as quickly as possible. The big cities had their own direct lines and we had to plug into a free line and ring once round the dial whilst holding the ring key back, to measure the length of the ring. This length of ring tone was necessary for the connection. Occasionally the ring key would stick causing an awful noise in the answering operator's ear. This happened to an operator sitting near to me and in a very dry voice she said – Nottingham, you ring once round the dial not twice round the switchroom.

Each morning girls on the early shift had to clean their board using a special soft bristle brush to sweep between the plugs and keys. Any dust went on the floor and the cleaners swept it up. Once a week, on Sundays I think, we would even polish the wood on our position. We also checked the tips of the plugs were not dirty or worn. If they were too bad we had to put a special sleeve on them and report them to the Faults operator. After a while an engineer would arrive to put everything in order.

If the tip of the plug was dirty and not registering an engaged line with a click it was possible to burn off the dirt by putting another plug tip to tip and ringing. This worked but made an awful smell so it wasn't encouraged.

Each call had to be charged so we had to learn how to do this either by the meter on the switchboard or by writing a ticket. When I came out of training I was issued with my own numbered headset. 84, and each ticket I made had to be initialled by that number.

The call boxes were identified by a red light and in those days we had to count out loud the money as it was put in. Each coin had a different sound and of course there was Button A to deposit the money and Button B to refund the money if the call couldn't be connected. The long distance calls were timed for three minutes and pips were sounded to the caller. We then had to go onto the line and say – Caller, your time is up. Do you wish to pay for further time? Sometimes the caller was lucky enough to get extra time if we were too busy to interrupt their call.

A caller could transfer the charge to the number they were calling and we had to ask if they would accept.

It was many years into my service when I was on duty one Sunday evening and I noticed that I was getting several calls from young boys booking transfer charge calls which were always refused. It dawned on me eventually that these boys were calling from a public school and it was their way of letting their parents know that they had arrived safely after weekend leave. Just by my asking them to accept the charge told them all was well. I was tempted to tell them I knew what they were doing but I didn't want to spoil their fun, and it was a clever dodge.

It was about the same time that young boys were making nuisance calls and one evening it was particularly irritating. I took one call, ignored what they were saying and left the plug in. We all did this hoping they would eventually give up. I then took another call and it was another group of boys so I connected them to each other without saying anything. It was very amusing to hear them trying to work out what was going on. However I digress.

We weren't allowed to operate on our own at first but had sessions sitting next to an experienced operator to listen to her dealing with the calls. Each operating position had a double jack so we could plug in without interrupting her work. Our training was mainly theory until near the end of the eight weeks. We were then put on a board and allowed to take calls. Either Miss T or a senior operator plugged in to supervise and correct us if we made any mistakes. This was quite scary at first and our first 'Number Please' was timid but we gained a degree of confidence and were soon considered able to be tested at the end of our training.

We were seated at a position and allowed to operate but after a while the Chief Supervisor came and plugged in to assess our ability as a junior telephonist. This was even more scary as the Chief, Miss Nobles, was held in awe by all. However I found during my time at the Exchange that although she was very strict she was also very kind and helpful if any operator had personal problems.

I think that the test lasted about half an hour but it felt longer. She then conferred with Miss T and we were told if we had passed. I was very happy that I had.

Girls of under 16 yrs old could be employed prior to reaching the age to be trained. They sat on a chair placed so that they could see most of the operators and their duties were to collect any tickets from the holder at the back of an operator's chair and take them to the delayed calls position. Every hour they had to collect all the tickets from the operators to take them to Accounts for sorting and pricing. They also were on hand to sharpen pencils. When they were old enough they started their training and I'm sure that their work as a junior helped them a lot as they had picked up on how the calls were dealt with which gave them a lot of confidence.

Junior operators were very much at the bottom of seniority and I had to learn how to defer to the older set. We had morning and afternoon breaks in the canteen but I couldn't speak to any seniors until they addressed me. I couldn't even sit at the same table as them unless invited.

I was accepted quite soon by most of them as my brother, Geoff, was a telephone engineer before joining the RAF and at that time was engaged to a senior operator.

When I reached the dizzy height of a senior operator I made a point of including juniors in our conversations.

One very strict rule was punctuality which was not a problem for me as I had been brought up never to be late for any appointment. We worked shift hours which could change from day to day so it was imperative to check your hours from the duty sheets. The first three minutes late was frowned on but allowed but after that a fine was imposed and deducted from the weekly wage. As my starting wage was less than £1 a fine was the last thing I wanted. We had to sign on and off duty and a supervisor was usually on hand to check that no one cheated.

I had been there for a number of years before I slipped up, misread my morning start and arrived at 8.30 am instead of 8 am. I was mortified.

On our breaks, if you were relieved for fifteen minutes it was exactly that, no rounding it up to the nearest five minutes.

If we found we needed a toilet break we had to ask a supervisor if we could 'go along'

Our late shift finished at eight or nine in the evening but the male night staff came in at 8 pm and we worked alongside them for the last hour.

We, the day staff, sometimes got short staffed and the night staff filled in some of our vacancies. They were slower, and much older, than us and not so good at timekeeping but we coped.

I was on a duty relieving for breaks and had to relieve one of the men. I plugged into his board saying brightly "Your relief Mr Todd". (His name was Mr Sweeney!) He was not amused by my unintentional error.

I progressed from junior operator up to acting supervisor when I married. After marriage girls had to lose seniority and so resign and return to the post of an ordinary operator.

My first year at the Exchange was the last year of the War and after gaining enough experience of the usual switchboard operating we had extra training on manning an emergency Exchange deep in a reinforced, underground shelter reached by underground passages.

This and other information we had access to was highly secret and we were always reminded that we were bound by the Official Secrets Act.

The Air Raid Warning system was routed through the Exchange and it was tested at 3 pm each afternoon heralded by an extremely loud buzzer.

Another priority call was a Royal connection and these had their own secrecy aid with a 'scrambler'. There was no way anyone could listen in to these calls as the conversation was garbled by this device. We had several of these calls which I believe were between Althorp House and Royal residences. Other calls from the Forces and some Police lines were also given priority.

It was a matter of pride to get calls connected as quickly as possible even though a lot of lines were damaged by air raids and we had to cope with hours of delay to London and other cities. We were supposed to connect using set routes as printed in files either on our board or obtained from the enquiry desk but we used to use unofficial routes to try to get a connection set up. It was called worming a call through. However, now and again we received recorded information "There is no communication to ....." and we would then know that the city/town had suffered a really bad raid. We knew that we had no hope of connecting to that area. A sobering thought and I hated having to tell the caller this news. Invariably they asked for details but we had to tell them that we had no information.

A blackboard above the Delayed calls position recorded how many hours delay there was on major cities which we could pass on to the caller who would then decide whether to have the call kept in hand or to cancel it.

Any engaged calls with no delay posted were kept in hand on the board and tried after five minutes then ten. If it was still engaged the ticket was sent to the Delay position. On an engaged call she would try at five minute intervals for half an hour and then interrupt the call to see if the called number would accept it.

It was very irritating to then find that the caller had re-booked and been connected earlier.

There was a button on each position which when depressed could access information from the Enquiry position re booked calls, or any other operating procedure. This could be open to misuse by two or more operators each depressing the button and arranging change of duties or other business with each other. Most supervisors would turn a blind eye to this unless it was very busy.

We had to be on our guard as Miss Nobles, our Chief, could listen in to any position from her desk and we had no way of knowing which one she was plugged in to.

During busy periods it was quite usual for an operator to have a full board and sit back so that the supervisor could see she couldn't take more calls. The supervisor would then call out any incoming calls on that position so that another operator could pick it up from the multiple board which was duplicated all round the room. Sometimes two operators would plug in together and when it was thought that each was dealing with the call, both would pull out leaving the subscriber still waiting.

I think one of the most amusing things that occasionally happened was when there was an electrical storm and every lamp on the switchboards lit up. It was an amazing sight and we had to wait until the engineers dealt with it. We then had to apologise to the many subscribers who had been kept waiting.

We had practise sessions wearing our specially adapted gas masks which were usually good for a laugh but woe betide any operator who had left theirs in their locker.

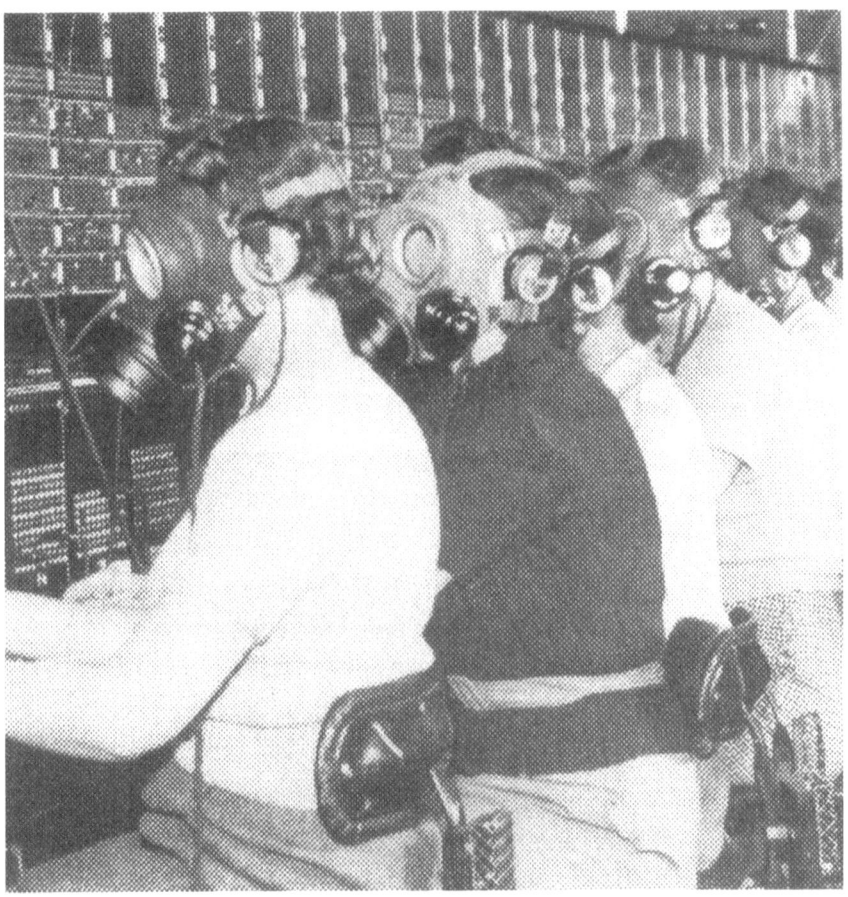

**Manning the switchboard wearing gas masks
with me at the front of the picture**

Part of the GPO Switchboard

In those days of manual switchboards each subscriber had a terminal on the board with its own little light, white ones for private lines and red ones for call boxes.

I hadn't long been out of training when I answered a red light coming from Wellingborough. It was my first experience of the 'F' word (at 16) and this awful caller told me what he wanted to do to me. I couldn't believe what I was hearing and resorted to the stock phrase "I'm sorry I didn't hear that. Will you repeat it?' So he did! I should have reported it to a supervisor but I was so shocked I just pulled the plug out. After that I always tried to avoid taking calls from a Wellingborough call box.

A number of the girls had boy friends or husbands in the Forces and had to be comforted when bad news came through. The Telegrams department was located in our building and one poor girl there was operating the teleprinter sending the message to the parents of her fiancé that he was missing, believed killed.

The messages from this department were delivered by Telegram Boys and people were usually afraid of bad news when they saw a boy at their door.

Someone in the Exchange heard it was possible to receive spirit messages using an Ouija board and as no board was available, all the letters in the alphabet were cut out plus the words yes and no. These were placed in a circle on one of the canteen tables with an upturned glass in the middle. A group of girls would each put one finger lightly on top of the glass and then questions would be asked of the 'spirit'. The glass would move to the letters to spell out answers to the questions, leading to accusing cries insisting that someone was moving the glass.

The craze caught on and soon girls were spending their relief breaks crowded round the table. It all got hilarious with outrageous questions asked and accusations and denials made. It was treated as a huge joke by most of us but unfortunately one girl, who obviously believed the spirits were present, asked questions about her soldier boy friend. For her last question she wanted to know if he would survive the war and fled in tears from the room when the glass went to 'No'. There was a shocked silence but having seen the reaction no one would admit making such a sick joke.

The sessions ended after that as we agreed that it could be too dangerous to dabble in such a game even though we had had a lot of fun with it.

All the rules and regulations made us into a close bunch and if any operator wanted a change of duty because of a boyfriend coming home on leave or for any other valid reason there was always someone who would oblige.

Our wages were paid in annual increments and as I said previously, mine started at the princely sum of just under £1 a week. I think it reached about £1.10s (£ 1. 50p) by the time I was 18 and I insisted on paying my board at home. Mum thought I still couldn't afford to but I paid her £1 and kept the rest as pocket money. I couldn't buy much with it but it had been my idea so I couldn't complain. I have to admit I was quite happy to work overtime when needed, to provide me with extra cash. Luckily for me overtime was allocated most weeks and as well as that, I could always volunteer to do other operator's overtime.

Geoff and Flora's wedding with me as a bridesmaid aged 18

Overtime could make a very long day for us as, for instance, a split shift of 8am to 12.30pm and 4pm to 8pm would often have 2pm to 4pm overtime added on. It was just as well that I enjoyed the work.

The only time I regretted having so little money was when I saw a coat I wanted in a shop window. I only had one coat which looked a bit odd over the longer length dresses that were coming into fashion. Mum offered to buy it for me but my pride wouldn't let me take up her offer so she lent me the money and I paid her back as soon as I was able.

Chapter 20

Victory in Europe and Peace in Northampton

When Victory came in 1945 and everyone wanted to call someone, the Exchange was like Blackpool Illuminations. We had no hope at all of giving swift service but luckily most of the callers were understanding and some commiserated with us at having to work at a time when everyone was out celebrating The telephonist sitting next to me was quite cross when, after advising the caller that there was no reply to her call, was told "You are not trying, I can see them in the garden". On the whole though it was quite an experience to be working on that day.

I was going out with a Pilot Officer stationed near Northampton at that time and he met me out of work when I finished at 8pm. He had a fellow officer with him who didn't want to be alone on such a momentous day so, of course, we asked him to join us. The three of us went for a meal in town and then joined in the festivities on the Market Square. When I got home, much later, I found that my brother Geoff, had managed to drive home for a few hours and he and Dad had formed a Victory "V" in our front garden using coloured Christmas tree lights. He also 'floodlit' me with his car headlights as my Pilot Officer kissed me goodnight at the corner of the street but we didn't care, it just made one more laugh in a very happy day.

A holiday club run in the Exchange helped me to budget for holidays. We decided the amount to pay weekly for the whole year but could take the total amount when needed. I think these clubs were run by the senior staff who also organised various trips to events out of town. One I particularly remember was to see Beniamino Gigli in concert at the De Montfort Hall in Leicester. He was considered the greatest tenor of that time and it certainly was a memorable experience to hear him sing.

His concerts were always a sell out and when we went, the only seats available, and affordable, were actually on the stage behind him. It didn't detract from enjoying his voice but we were delighted when he turned round and sang just for us. We gave him a great round of applause both before he sang as well as after. He really was a charming performer.

There were other quite varied trips organised which included visits to ice hockey matches at the Wembley Stadium in London. I went on one of these although I didn't know much about the game. It was winter and the weather had been extremely harsh with a lot of snow leaving the roads very icy. I wasn't feeling well at all but I had paid for the trip and didn't want to waste the money. The coach was leaving from Campbell Square and as there was no bus to get me there I set off to walk. As I crossed one road I slipped on the ice and fell heavily. I wasn't injured in any way but I felt so ill it would have been very easy to have sat there and burst into tears. However I picked myself up and went on my way to join the rest of the party. I perked up during the journey as we practised out chants for our favoured team and sang out

Two, Four, Six, Eight
Who do we appreciate
L I O N S - Lions.

Of course we chanted this at the stadium from our ringside seats, very near the ice so of course so I got more shivery as the game went on. The coach had no heating and ice coated the inside of the windows. It wasn't surprising that, after enduring all that cold and ice, I went down with a severe case of bronchitis and needed a few weeks off sick from work to get over it.

Another event we attended was to a Dance at the nearby Sywell Aerodrome at the invitation of the French airmen stationed there. They provided a coach to and from the aerodrome. I was still the youngest girl in the Exchange and the older girls warned me to take care to stay in the hall and never agree to go to see their quarters.

Looking back it is quite funny as in later years I was to meet and eventually marry a Frenchman.

As I gained more experience at work I was promoted to manning the Enquiry desk where we dealt with a variety of tasks. The obvious was finding telephone numbers for callers and we had a huge number of Directories which weren't available to the public.

There were set expressions to use for this: The first was 'Which town please?' then 'What name please?' and finally 'What initial please?' Imagine my confusion when the name was Soul and the initial was R especially as we had to repeat the information back to the caller to make sure we were looking in the right place!

There were special lines for the operators asking for routing and cost of trunk calls to long distant exchanges not included in their files.

We were the first stop for callers asking for a supervisor and it was our job then to sort out the problem for them but if it was more serious and the caller was extremely cross and abusive we would transfer the call to the Exchange supervisor.

During evenings and weekends we would get a lot of doctors ringing to arrange for their calls to be transferred to a doctor on call. During one Friday evening I was getting these requests one after another and out of curiosity I sat and worked through the chain of transfers to find out which doctors were actually on call for that weekend. I was amazed, and horrified, to find that it came down to just one doctor taking all the calls from Northampton. I wonder if he realised!

Another job that came with seniority was the chance to go to the small exchanges of Daventry or Towcester when one of their three or four operators was on sick or holiday leave. I only went to Towcester once which I didn't enjoy. Although I was senior to all of them they knew the work better and resented having a 'stranger' put in charge of them. I won them over by putting it to them that, as I didn't know a lot about the working of their Exchange it would be better if they carried on as they usually did and helping me out when needed.

The most amusing thing there was the Emergency Fire calls. Once the alarm came into the Exchange the siren had to be activated to call out the firemen. It was amusing to look out of the window and see the firemen scurrying to the Fire Station which was near to the Exchange. These were a Volunteer Force that had to down tools at their jobs and get to the Station as soon as they could. The fire engines couldn't go out until all the men had arrived.

It reminded me of a comedian, Rob Wilton, when he did a send up of being a fireman. He answered the phone, very slowly taking the details of the fire. He finished the call saying "Don't worry," we'll be leaving soon so keep it going until we get there".

It was much more enjoyable to go to Daventry Exchange.

In those days the Exchange was housed in a small room above the Post Office in Sheaf Street,and was manned by Miss Mabel N, Ms Connie P and Mrs Millie R. There was just one male operator to cover the night shift from 8pm to 8am. There were three switchboards of the old-fashioned 'eyeball' type. When a subscriber in Daventry town lifted the receiver the round metal plate eyeball would drop to reveal which number was calling and would go back out of view once the receiver was replaced. It was all very different to the system I was used to at Northampton.

It was quite daunting arriving at Daventry to introduce myself to the staff. They were quite wary of a new face and it took a little time for them to accept me but after a while they did and were very helpful in initiating me into the workings of the small community that was Daventry at that time numbering just under 4,000 inhabitants and with only about 200 telephone subscribers. The first thing I had to get used to was that most callers didn't ask to be connected to a local number. When answered by "Number please?" they would say something like "Put me through to Mrs ??", or even "Do you know if Mrs ?? is in this morning?". Millie and Connie knew all the subscribers comings and goings so I was really grateful for their prompting but I had to quickly learn who was who in the town. The whole atmosphere was extremely informal, so different to the rigid type of operating at Northampton but once I was accepted it was a lot of fun.

Connie was especially amusing as although she was middle-aged with a grown up son, she had the voice of a young girl and used to delight in chatting and sometimes even making dates with service men from nearby camps. She had no intention of meeting them of course, sometimes making a date was the only way of getting them off the line, as most operators found.

We had meal breaks, morning coffee and biscuits were taken in the switchroom as was afternoon tea and biscuits but I went out for lunch to the British Restaurant which was a communal Government run eating establishment. It was in a hall near to the Roman Catholic Church in New Street and a substantial hot meal, consisting of meat with veg. followed by a pudding, was provided for a shilling (5p). There were always plenty of customers, probably most were from the shops and factories but some were house holders. The meal was very good value for the money, a similar meal at the other restaurants in Daventry would probably have cost about 2 shillings and sixpence (26½p).

The day staff worked shifts to cover the hours from 8am to 8pm and the worst one for me was the split shift – 9am to 12.30 and 4pm to 8pm. This left a boring gap in the afternoon, as there wasn't a lot to do in Daventry in those days. I was quite pleased therefore when the telephone engineer invited me to go out on his calls with him. He went out to the outlying villages to repair telephones reported out of order and I would stay in the van while he went in to fix them. Occasionally he would take me in with him and introduce me as his assistant, usually this was at the 'big' houses such as the manor house in Ashby St Ledgers. It was there that the butler led us to the boudoir in order to repair Viscountess's telephone. It was probably breaking lots of rules but it was very interesting and these outings helped to pass what would have been some tedious hours.

Bill, the night operator, worked from 8pm to 8am the next morning. He lived on the floor below the switchroom and was supposed to come up ten minutes early to give me time to get to the bus stop to catch the 8pm bus home. Unfortunately he didn't always remember and I had to go down to remind him so it was always a scramble to catch the bus. If I missed it the next bus was the last one, an hour later.

There was a United Counties bus strike one day which left the only way to get to Daventry was by train. At Northampton station I got on the train to change at Weedon for Daventry. On the train from Weedon I soon realized I was on the wrong train and was told by other passengers it was going non-stop to Rugby. I was glad that I'd got talking to a girl who was trying to get to a factory in Daventry so we were both in the same predicament and also found we had both been misinformed by the porter at Weedon.

When we arrived at Rugby we had to work out how to get back to Daventry. Luckily the Midland Red buses were not on strike and we found the right bus.

I rang the Exchange to tell them what had happened and to say I would be there eventually. It was nearly lunch time when I arrived and I had to go down to see the Head Postmaster to fill in a form explaining what had happened.

I was relieved to find the United Counties buses were back to normal by the time I went home and were still running normally the next day.

The thing I found most difficult to do was claiming subsistence to cover the cost of travelling and meals.

I got a season ticket from the bus company which gave a much cheaper price but other operators who also went out on relief said I must claim a single fare to and from Daventry which was much more expensive. When I objected to this practice they told me that I had to conform or I would be letting them down.

It was a similar thing claiming back the cost of meals. Instead of the actual price of a shilling (5 pence) at the British restaurant I had to charge 2/6 (22½ p). I felt extremely guilty doing this and hated filling in the necessary form to get it signed by the Head Postmaster. He probably knew what went on but never queried it.

At Northampton I was promoted to the Accounts Department, actually two large tables in a corner of the Exchange, where all the calls were charged and sorted. It was pleasant work but my real love was for the hands-on switchboard.

Now the war was over some luxuries were appearing in the shops and if the word went round that beauty products were on sale in the Town Centre we girls on Accounts became errand girls. Officially we weren't allowed to leave the building without permission so one girl volunteered, or was delegated, to take a chance and pop out in her refreshment break. She then collected a shopping list for the goodies we'd heard were available.

I remember going to McKinnells, a nearby chemist one day with an order for several tubs of Yardley talcum powder and another time for Max Factor pancake make - up.

I found out that there was a small sweet shop belonging to a lady who made her own boiled sweets. Sweets were still rationed but for some reason hers were off rations. The shop was on my way home so I was always the messenger for buying them. I had to give up some of my lunchtime for that but it was worth it and many an afternoon the accounts staff sorted the tickets happily sucking on clove or treacle toffees, mint humbugs and other delicious sweets.

I was further promoted to the Clerical desk but didn't enjoy that work at all. I found it boring and I quickly learned that it was possible to take a walk in the building as long as you carried a file or something else that looked important.

It was while I was on Clerical that it was decided the standard expressions telephone operators had used for many years could now be replaced by more friendly greetings and expressions. Of course 'Number Please' stayed but an operator could use her discretion how she informed a caller of the progress or inability to connect the call. I thought to myself that this could be fun, and when the phone rang I answered with a bright 'Good morning, this is the clerical department in Northampton Telephone Exchange. Can I help you?' I think I dressed it up even more but I can't remember my exact words, probably because of the shock I felt when I was answered by Miss Nobles, our Chief. She said 'Very nice Miss Britten, (how did she know it was me?) I think you can'.

I think I had a reputation of being the clown of the office as one day a group of us was laughing about something I'd said when a Supervisor came by and said that whenever there was a group laughing it was usually me in the middle.

It was pleasant to get permission to leave the Exchange during a meal break as the town was always bustling and it was possible to spot some of the town's characters. The most easily recognizable was the Coroner, Mr Pat Darnell. He looked quite Edwardian wearing his top hat, a flowing frock coat and always had a pipe in his mouth.

The twins of the Beverley Sisters were evacuated to Northampton and later worked at the Chronicle and Echo offices on the corner of the Market Square. They too were noticeable as they always walked arm in arm and dressed identically, often in camel coats with a red blouse showing.

In America my brother Geoff had qualified as a pilot in Arizona, and now came back to England. He was engaged to a girl in our exchange when he left but he had met and fallen in love with a local girl named Flora, in Mesa –Arizona, while training there. He therefore had to call off his engagement. He asked me not to discuss it with anyone at the exchange for her sake and of course I didn't intend to as I felt so sorry for her. Needless to say it caused a sensation at work and the senior staff, especially, tried really hard to make me talk about it. It wasn't an easy time for me as well as her and I think she left after a while.

Flora came to join Geoff in England and the local Press found out about their plans and came to interview them. They took pictures and wanted one of Flora enjoying a cup of English tea which couldn't happen as Flora was, and still is, a Mormon. Her religion forbids taking stimulants which includes tea, so she was photographed drinking milk!

It was at the time when a lot of girls were marrying Americans and leaving to make their life in America. They were dubbed GI Brides and the Press decided to call Flora a GI Bride in reverse which wasn't popular with any of us.

Geoff and Flora married at Abington Church in March 1946 and I was Flora's only bridesmaid. They had to live with us in Baring Road and their first child, Alan, was born in 1947.

When Flora went into labour during the evening prior to Alan's birth, they had to battle through a heavy snow storm to get to the Maternity hospital. Geoff had to leave her there, as was usual in those days, he came home again with instructions to ring in the morning. The snow storm continued all through the night and we had to dig a path through the deep snow before we could get out of the house. We had no phone so Geoff had to struggle up to the call box at the top of the street. He came back beaming with the news of his first son and we were all so happy.

It couldn't have been easy for them to look after Alan as it was very cramped in the house with all of us but eventually they were lucky enough to rent a Pre-fab in Northampton, one of many which had been built, or rather assembled, in and around the town. Although they were prefabricated the interiors were well appointed. They were, of course, thankful to move into a home of their own.

When Geoff was demobbed he came back to take up his post as a GPO telephone engineer. His job had been kept for him as the Government had decreed that all men who joined the Forces would have their jobs back after the war. Geoff didn't find it easy to go back to work with men who hadn't joined up and were promoted over him. He was suddenly junior to younger men. Although he was far from happy in his work he stuck it until 1951 when he left Northampton with Flora and his son to go to live in America. I was devastated at having to say goodbye to them. Geoff and I hugged each other and found it hard to let go. It was to be the last time I saw him as he died in 1966, aged only 42.

The winter of 1946/47 was very harsh with extremely heavy snow covering the ice beneath. The roads were bad and the buses weren't able to keep to timetables so, like most people I walked to and from work and anywhere else I needed to go. Most shopkeepers and householders did their best to keep their patch of pavement cleared. We did at home and also put down ashes at the front of the house to try to cut down the risk of slipping. Many people wore thick socks over their shoes which made walking a bit safer but as it snowed or froze almost every day until mid March lots of socks were worn out.

Rivers and lakes were frozen hard and people who were lucky enough to have ice skates were soon on the ice having a great time. The not so lucky people, like me, also went on the ice to just slide and have fun.

A couple of my work mates had a sledge each and one evening a group of us went to a hill on the outskirts of Northampton where we had great fun riding the sledges to the bottom, about three to each sled. We could only try to steer using our shoes and often finished up in the snow drift at the side of the run. As the sledge tipped when it hit the drift we landed on top of each other. We were the only people out and it was a clear moonlit night, really beautiful in the snow. I still cherish the memory. We stayed there until quite late and then had a hot drink at the house of one of the group, not that we were at all cold after all the exertion.

A group of us loved dancing and we went regularly to the Salon on Saturday nights. We always had a good time and enjoyed both the dancing and the dance bands. We were lucky that Northampton had some really good dance bands at that time. When there was a drum break in the music the dancers would stop and gather round to listen, applauding loudly when the drummer had finished his solo. For an ordinary Saturday night dance there was just one band playing on the stage and at the interval, when the band left for refreshments, records were played. For a mid week or special dance there were two bands.

A lot of Americans from their Air Force camps came to the dances and they were very nice, always polite. Their uniforms were so smart too. A colleague from work was going out with an American officer who got her enough uniform material to have a suit made. It was in the olive green colour of the jacket and the suit looked beautiful. A lot of us were quite envious of her coupon free outfit.

During one of the dances a coloured airman asked me to dance. I had never met a black fellow before and I'm ashamed to say I went all shy and said I was sitting the dance out. I must have hurt him and I regret it to this day. After I had refused him I went to the ladies cloakroom so that I didn't get asked by any other fellow. My guilt really spoilt the evening which served me right.

Chapter 21

Romance and Separation

On October 18th 1947 I went to the usual Saturday dance at the Salon and had a great time with lots of partners. I went with Jean, a girl from work but we only met up between dances and at the interval. When the last waltz started I saw the two men coming towards us. The one I had previously danced with reached me first, as I hoped he would, and we danced. As was the custom the last partner you had would ask to see you home which he did but when I found out that he had to go back to Daventry in a car with his friends I insisted he only took me halfway. He went but not before he made a date to meet me to go to the cinema, or to the pictures as it was usually called then.

It was arranged for the next Wednesday and Mum was very surprised to know that I was looking forward to it. She was more used to me making dates and then wishing I hadn't. I told her that his name was Marcel and that he was French.

Wednesday came and I made my way to the Market Square as agreed but there was no sign of Marcel. I waited and waited but he didn't come and feeling very disappointed to think he had not arrived I walked away towards the cinema. To my surprise I met Marcel halfway along to find that he'd been waiting for me on the other side of the square. We were both relieved to see each other and went into the cinema to enjoy the film, Mildred Pierce, and each other's company.

We met again often, mostly to go dancing and sometimes to the pictures but we made sure we knew exactly where we were meeting!

He was living with his parents at Gresham House in Sheaf Street so I was happy to be sent over to Daventry Exchange any time I was needed, in fact I often volunteered.

Before I met him it was a scramble to catch the 8pm bus back to Northampton when I was on the late shift. However, after I met Marcel I used to stay on in Daventry until the 9pm bus, which was I believe was the last bus back. We would stroll round the town getting to know each other better. We would meet during the daytime too whenever possible, and one day Marcel's father saw us walking along hand in hand. He was furious and told Marcel that it was disgraceful behaviour!

The family was all returning to France to live six weeks from our first meeting and one evening, just three weeks after we met, we were walking through the churchyard prior to me catching the 9pm bus and Marcel asked me to marry him. I said yes but we agreed that he would come back from France at Easter and if we still felt the same way then, we would become engaged.

I had already been to his house to meet his parents and to have a meal with them so I had to ask him home to meet my parents. I asked Mum if he could come for a meal and when she hesitated I added that she ought to say yes as he wanted to marry me. She took it quite well really!

We saw each other often before he left and when he had gone I missed him a lot. I didn't tell anyone about the Easter arrangement just in case we didn't feel the same so I didn't talk about him to friends and colleagues which was a secret hard to keep.

I filled my time with going to dances and the 'pictures'. Luckily I had a good circle of friends although the girl I had always considered to be my best friend wouldn't go out with me at all. It was strange really and she didn't give me a reason for refusing, in fact, she hardly spoke to me at all. I came to the conclusion that she was jealous of my meeting Marcel but I couldn't imagine why.

I often went to dances with Joyce who was a lot of fun to be with. She was a very attractive girl who had long, thick, wavy blonde hair. She wasn't fond of her hair though and on hot days and after dancing a lot at the Salon the back of her dress was dark with sweat caused by the weight of her hair.

Butlins Holiday camps were very popular at this time and a Butlins Social Club was formed in Northampton run by an older couple. Joyce and I joined along with a group from work and we all enjoyed the regular meetings and days out to the Butlins Camp at Skegness and other places.

Butlin's Holiday Camp with me kneeling in front of Jean W and another girl

In my best finery at Butlins

These activities as well as other trips from work made the time pass pleasantly, if not quickly enough, until Easter.

I was excited at the thought of seeing Marcel again but a little apprehensive wondering if he still felt the same, I knew I did,

I met him at the station and once we were together any doubts went and we looked forward to getting formally engaged the next day, Easter Saturday.

In the morning we went into town to buy the ring and came back to the room where Marcel was staying in Franklins Gardens Hotel where he put the ring on my finger. We then went home to show it to Mum and Dad and from there round to relatives to spread the good news. Everyone was happy for us and, of course, we were on Cloud Nine.

The day we got engaged

The weekend passed too quickly and we soon had to say goodbye again. Marcel had broken it to me that when he got back he would have to go into the Army. When he had gone to renew his passport before coming to England the officials said he couldn't leave the country as he hadn't done his National Service. He pleaded his case and in the end they gave him a short pass but said he would be called up on his return. This meant that we were saying goodbye not knowing how long it would be before we could be together again.

It made it doubly hard to say goodbye in the early hours of the morning after the Easter holiday.

Our engagement was greeted with surprise when I went back to work with most of them saying they didn't know I was going out with anyone. That was how well I had kept my secret.

Marcel hadn't been back very long before he was called up into the French Army, as he had been warned. Letters passed frequently between us, in fact, we wrote almost every day.

Marcel in the 33rd Artillery Regiment

I worked with a girl who was engaged to a French airman and when we were together we tried to converse in French and it went quite well.

Once again I kept myself busy with work and socializing. Four of us went on holiday to Torquay. I have a photo taken by a street photographer of us walking out, three of us in trousers and me in shorts which was considered a bit daring. Women had started wearing trousers during the war in the Forces and in factories but not many women were wearing them in the street.

Another time just two of us went to Porlock which was beautiful and we enjoyed the lovely scenery and the beach. There was an ice cream café on the edge of the beach where we sampled and enjoyed a delicious Knicker Bocker Glory. I think they cost about 2/6 (12½ p) which was a lot of money for us then. We went back several times but nothing quite equalled that first taste.

One evening we went to the beach after sunset and as we walked towards the sea we heard music coming from a nearby house. The owner was playing a record and we stood on the beach in bright moonlight listening to the finale of Grieg's Piano Concerto – magic!

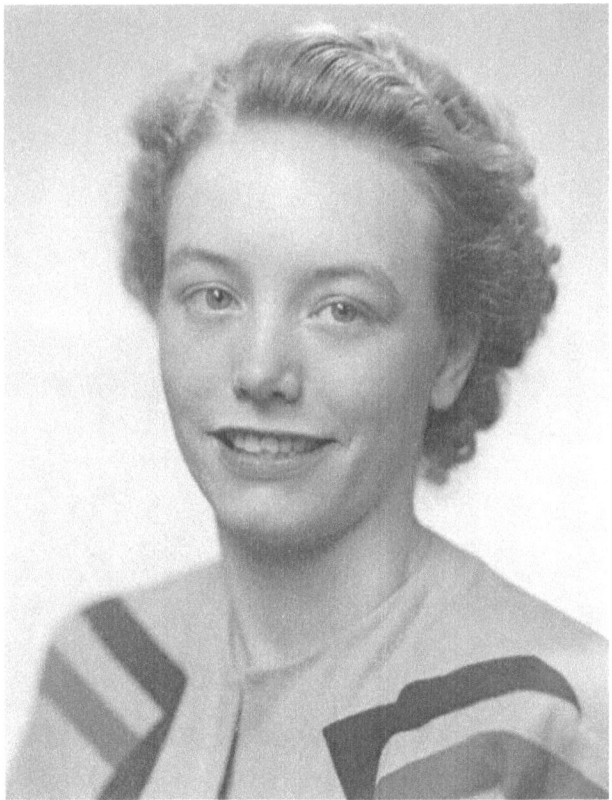

Molly aged 20

On another day we went for a walk in the fields on a hill. We took a rest in a meadow full of buttercups and daisies and lay in the hot sunshine. When we decided to move we got out onto the road and as we went down the steep incline we realized we were on the famous Porlock Hill. We had meant to go there on another day because we had found it by accident and as it was so steep we decided to forego walking uphill.

A large group of us from the exchange got together for bike rides, usually at the weekends but sometimes in the evenings. A favourite ride was through Salcey Forest as there were different routes we could take. During the weekend rides we would stop at a café in the forest for refreshments. On one visit we took photos and we all piled on to a rustic bench, some sitting and others sitting on the back of the bench. The girl taking the photo was just about to snap us when the bench started sinking into the grass with the weight of us and then toppled over depositing us all in a heap. It must have looked a comical sight but alas the photo opportunity was missed because we were all helpless with laughter. Luckily the bench wasn't damaged.

Our cycling group at Salcey Forest, with me second from the left

I enjoyed a game of tennis so when my friend Joyce asked me if I'd like to make up a foursome one evening, I was happy to agree. I found out that her boyfriend at that time was an Army officer stationed at the local barracks and it was one of his fellow officers I was to play with.

They met us at the entrance to allow us to go in and we had some good games of tennis until the light faded.

Joyce then went off with her boyfriend and left me with the other fellow. He asked me back to his quarters for a drink which I thought would be coffee but it was an alcoholic drink he served. Like a naïve idiot I accepted which he took to be a prelude to kissing and wanting to go further I dodged the kiss and searched my mind for a way to leave. Luckily his batman came in and while he was in the room I said that it was getting late and, thanking him for the game, made my escape. He was not pleased and I left behind a very grumpy officer.

When I saw Joyce the next day I told her what had happened and said I was annoyed with her for leaving me alone with an officer who was certainly not a gentleman!

The end of 1948 was a sad time for our family as a week before Christmas Nan Britten died. As I mentioned earlier she had Pagets disease so her death was expected but was still sad. Then on December 23rd came the unexpected death of my much loved Papa Ives.

I was at home with Mum when Aunt Norah came to fetch Mum as she said Papa had been taken seriously ill. They dashed off and I had to tell Dad when he came home from work who also hurried off. I was left feeling upset and very apprehensive.

Mum and Dad came home much later and told me he had died quite suddenly in his chair whilst enjoying the pre-Christmas visit of his sisters. He leaned forward to throw his cigarette butt into the fire and fell back dead. He died at once but Aunt Norah didn't tell us that. I think she must have been afraid of our reaction. We were all devastated.

The funeral was arranged for the day after Boxing Day. In those days it was usually three days after a death. I had to put in a written request to the Postmaster asking for leave on that day. Miss Nobles called me over before I left the switchroom and said she was so sorry but she had to ask me if my request was genuine. The Postmaster had queried it because I had already had a day off to attend my grandmother's funeral just before Christmas. I understood that it did look suspicious but she was so kind when I assured her that I would never use such an excuse to get time off.

I went straight up to Nan's after work on Christmas Eve and I had been worrying most of the day about what I could say to her but when I saw her, so little, sitting in his chair, I found I didn't need words. I just went to her and put my arms round her and we hugged each other tightly. She was even trying to comfort me saying she knew how much I loved him.

Of the many happy memories I have of him was that I was in the habit of seeing Nan and Papa each Saturday evening before going to a dance. Papa would always go into his garden and pick a flower for me to wear. It was often a small rose bud but he always found something for me.

He was a lovely man and it seemed strange that I was a little afraid of him when I was little. He had a large moustache during my early childhood and one day I was visiting with Mum when Papa came home from work without the moustache. I hardly recognised him and I remember him being amused at my fright as I cowered in Mum's lap.

When I was older I was never scared of him and we used to have great fun together as I usually teased him lots and could always make him laugh.

I went to see Papa in his coffin which had been put in the front room. I had never seen a dead body before but he didn't frighten me, how could he? The only thing that did bother me was that he had been put in a white satin shirt which had a mandarin neckline. It was silly of me but I felt he would have hated to be dressed like that. However, it was the norm then, no one was buried in their own clothes.

On the day of the funeral the undertakers came to close the coffin and it upset all of us to hear them hammering in the nails. I gulped down a sob and was promptly thumped by Mum and told, " Don't you dare cry".

I remember a lot of things in my life but I have to confess that I don't remember anything of the funeral other than Papa was cremated.

Bodies to be cremated were put into mauve coffins but I don't think Papa was put in one of those.

After the out of town relatives had left I stayed with Nan for several days until she said she thought she could cope with being alone. I was reluctant to leave her even then as I slept with her during my stay and had heard her sobbing herself to sleep.

I didn't take it too well either and had nightmares of Papa getting out of his coffin still dressed in that awful outfit.

It took a while to get over the shock of his death which was made harder because Christmas was being celebrated around us. However we had to adjust and life settled down to a slightly different pattern. I tried to visit Nan as often as possible and go for walks with her. We walked for miles and she took me to parts of Abington and Weston Favell I had never been to before. She started to come to us every Sunday for tea and never missed even in pouring rain. She always walked and if we expressed surprise at her venturing out she would always say that it wasn't raining when she set out. It got to be quite a catch phrase for us.

The time passed and I still didn't know when Marcel was coming back and frequent letters were exchanged between us. French Army personnel had very little pay during their service so they had to rely on parents for money. Marcel's parents had emigrated to South Africa while he was in the Army and left him with nothing except his piano, which he had to sell.

His uncles who both lived in Paris were very good to him and looked after him on his leaves and made sure he had money in his pocket but it wasn't a nice situation for him.

Marcel was able to share good news with me when the Army decreed that any personnel who were previously living abroad could be demobbed earlier. Sure enough he came out of the Army but still couldn't come over at once because he couldn't afford it. He went into digs and got a job in the North of France until he could gather enough money although he was only allowed to bring £5 with him.

He wasn't allowed to enter the country unless he had an address and a job to come to so I had to sort that out for him. He would be lodging with Nan which would be a help for her too.

I arranged to see the Personnel Manager at the Express Lift Company and told him of Marcel's experience as a draughtsman and also explained that he had to have the offer of a job to be able to come to live in Northampton.

On the strength of what I'd told him he very kindly agreed to employ Marcel after interviewing him on arrival.

My 21st birthday was in March and we were happy to look forward to his arrival in time for the planned party.

The details were sorted out for the party, invitations sent and food arranged. Dried fruits and butter etc were still rationed and we were wondering if I would be able to have a celebration cake. Mum had told our grocery supplier that it she thought it would be difficult to get the ingredients together. He took her to one side and said to her "Don't worry, let me have the recipe and I'll supply what you need". He was well known in the area, and by the police, for supplying food off the ration. He used to laugh and say – look at those plain clothes police over the road, they're trying to catch me out. He was a good hearted villain though and never let anyone go short. In the case of my cake, rightly or wrongly Mum went along with it and the cake was made.

The one sad thing that marred the occasion was that Papa, who had always decorated our Christmas and Birthday cakes, of course would not be able to do mine. Nan gave me 21 guineas, one for each year of my life and signed the card from both of them.

Mum and Dad had hired the Hall for the party and Geoff asked what music was planned. He was horrified with the sedate music they had chosen and said it should be much livelier. He went out to buy more records and one of them which I'll never forget was "Cigareets and Whisky and Wild Wild Women".

Marcel arrived the day before the party and so made it a double celebration.

I received a lot of nice presents and cards and the whole occasion was a happy gathering.

After the weekend Marcel and I enjoyed being together again and began to look forward to our wedding. We had no money because of Marcel's limited allowance to bring out of France and I had very little in the way of savings because of my low wages. We decided to set a date because, as mentioned earlier, I had now worked at the GPO for six years and so was eligible to apply for the Marriage Dowry. This would amount to nearly £100 which was a big help

The date we eventually decided on was 22nd April 1950 .... but that's another story.

www.ingramcontent.com/pod-product-compliance
Lightning Source LLC
Chambersburg PA
CBHW020420290526
45785CB00002B/658